HOUSE HACKING

USING RENOVATION LOANS FOR A BETTER WAY TO BUY A HOME

JOHN DAVID ADAMS, JR.

Paperback ISBN: 979-8-9864719-0-7
Digital ISBN: 979-8-9864719-1-4
Connect with John David Adams, Jr
Website: www.thehousehackingbook.com
Email: thehousehackingbook@gmail.com

DEDICATION

The only reason we get to enjoy a home to safely live and create wealth in, is because a soldier has been willing to put it all on the line for our freedom.

Freedom isn't free, it is costly. There are people out there paying the price every day for us to live here in the greatest country in the world. When trouble calls, they leave their families, businesses, and livelihood to defend it and we must not forget those who serve.

It is with a passion to esteem those who have served and honor them in a special way, that I dedicate this book to the men and women that defend our nation. The profits generated by this book will be used to help end veteran suicide by donations to K9s For Warriors and Cross the Line Foundation veteran charities. I believe in their mission and hope you will consider helping them as well. I do this to honor the fallen and veterans with invisible scars. Your service means so much to me!

ACKNOWLEDGEMENTS

My struggle with ADHD made writing this book one of the most difficult things I have ever done. It has taken not only my time, talent, blood, tears and sweat but other's as well.

Without the support of my wife Stephanie and family I wouldn't have pushed to do this! They kept me going when I wanted to quit.

I am thankful for the self-help and motivational books that gave me the courage to start.

Robert Tait, your story inspired me to get off my butt and hire someone to help me put this together.

You introduced me to our publisher Kim Thompson-Pinder and her team from RTI Publishing and for that I am grateful as they have been amazing.

Adam Smith, If it wasn't for your mastermind, I wouldn't have seen Robert talk!

Ron Byrom – You are a great renovation loan officer and leaned on you heavily for a lot of technical in my book. We have worked together as colleagues but have been more than just a friend.

You also helped me identify an issue with my son's vision early on, so he didn't go blind .... I could write a book about that. Your heart and brotherly love have been much appreciated.

Gina Troglia – Thanks for all you do to support my operations in the renovation space and always ironing it out for the customer and the detailed info we needed to get right in the disbarment section of this book.

Midge, John Sway, Dustin Swigart, John Elian and Patti Kimbrough you are also top-notch renovation specialists and have graciously help me add great accounts of clients that have used the power of renovation lending to change and shape lives of our borrowers and their generations.

To my right hands at work Maryann, Tu, John and Mike ... you guys have always had my back and will always have yours. I can't take all the credit for the work we have done in the last 20 years as you have been right there beside me living in the trenches of these customers stories.

From the bottom of my heart, I also want to thank every one of my customers. THEIR trust, patience. and belief in me not only allowed me to get them into a better home but also provided for mine and I get to live what I am passionate about. These loans aren't easy, and I appreciate you allowing me to shepherd you through that process.

IF I missed anyone, know that I appreciate you and from the bottom of my heart, thank you.

Table of Contents

PROLOGUE

In early 2015, the search began for the right home that would be great for me to renovate and sell.

We purchased a foreclosure with renovations before for my father and somewhat knew the conventional method involved for financing but the difficult path that came next, I did not expect.

A search for homes in my price range landed me in another foreclosure. This time instead of it being a small cookie cutter house in town, I had found a 40-acre horse ranch with a 3,150 sq ft two-story home less than a mile from a beautiful lake in the country! It needed a lot of work compared to my last project, but I knew I was up to the task!

There was termite damage, the roof had to be replaced, all 3 A/C units were shot, the 1600 sq ft wooden deck was rotted and falling apart, and EVERYTHING needed updating. That was just the initial look…

Feeling optimistic that I could haggle the price down, I began my search for a lender familiar with VA lending. I got on the VA's website and went through the lending handbook and noticed there was a product for renovating a home by rolling the cost of repairs and upgrades into your final loan in addition to the purchase price of the home! Perfect, now where do I get this loan?

I called all the big banks, credit unions, and used a few websites that said they offered VA products, but none of them had even heard about a renovation loan product backed by the VA.

Everyone else that I talked to told me that to use a VA product the house had to be perfect and move-in ready and obviously the house I wanted was anything but!

At this point, I was getting very frustrated, and the clock was ticking! Someone was going to scoop up my dream home!

I kept looking and tried one last website, John Adams. It seemed kind of cheesy, but at this point I was desperate. I called the number and was able to talk directly to John Adams. He was friendly to speak to and was confident that we could do a VA Renovation loan! (Even though I found out later it had never been done on a Freddie Mac foreclosure before!)

My prayers were answered!

John gave me the giant list of things to do, and I got to work. It was way more than I expected. What was I thinking! This was nuts! John and I got into a few arguments along the way, mostly because I thought I knew everything about how renovating a home goes. Boy was I wrong. Inspections, Contractors, Quotes, you name it. I had bitten off more than I could chew! 90 days to complete all the repairs? This is never going to happen!

But…

With John guiding me along this arduous path, I was able to get all that I needed together. The loan was funded!!!

I found a General Contractor willing to work with me and get all the required repairs completed (almost) on time. Through all the pain and grumbling I did, John never lost hope.

Now my family and I have a 3,150 sq ft house on a beautiful 40-acre horse ranch that has been renovated and updated by using my VA Backed Home Loan.

John Adams closed my loan and I have re-financed with a cash-out refinancing and was able to borrow an additional$ 50,000 for building a 30x60 shop to house my farm equipment in addition to lowering my interest rate.

I would never have gotten this far without John Adams and his dedicated team. I consider this man family with all he has done for us!

John's knowledge is what made this possible and I am so glad that he is sharing it with you on this book.

Thanks again for making my dreams come to fruition!!!

Tom Osborn

PREFACE

"A dream does not become reality through magic; it takes sweat, determination, and hard work."
~ Colin Powell

The Crash Of 2008

Back in 2008, I learned a few hard lessons from my experience with real estate. Lots of people did and in that, I'm not unique. However, with what I have been through, I was able to start myself on the way to recovery to hacking homes for profit, and helping others do the same. I've gone from bankruptcy to being a millionaire in real estate. My new resolve and mission in life are to help you make better decisions than I did. That is why I hope you are reading this book. Allow me to show you how I have found a better way to buy a home.

Before all of that, in the earlier 2000s, I was an engineer and I had gone down the path of buying a home several times, but I was reluctant to do so and failed to commit after several attempts. I'm a geriatric millennial—by virtue, we are lumped into a mass of a generation that is scared to make decisions or the wrong decision, so I was never able to close on anything at that point in my life. I overthought everything.

I got my real estate license, thinking that would help, and even took the Carlton H Sheets real estate program offered on a TV infomercial to kind of bone up on how to do real estate. Incidentally, that was the highest-selling infomercial product on TV ever, and Carlton made more money on that program than real estate! We will talk about that in the closing chapter of this book.

My experience through the crash was that even though I did all that, I still didn't know what I was doing. I would try to buy homes that were in distress and fix them up, but I ended up spending too much on them and without an equity position. So, when the market turned, I lost all of the properties I worked so hard to keep. I went from indecision to wrong decision with false confidence in real estate, to financial ruin.

This may sound eerily like what is going on today, but it is two different markets. If I would have done things a little differently from what I will describe in this book, then I would have come out of it in a much better position and may not have lost any of my property. The reason I want to share what I and my clients have done is because I have gone from bankruptcy to Millionaire and helped a lot of people do the same thing you can too without fancy seminars!

I am also borrowing input and some experience from a few other renovation mortgage specialists around the country who dedicated a large part of their business to renovation. In the following pages, they will lend their stories and expertise for your benefit. We will hear from some of their clients' success stories as well.

John S.

"I started as a regular retail loan officer for a mortgage company in San Diego. I was heavily focused on the VA market in North County San Diego and doing a lot of FHA loans. I became a specialist in financing HUD REO properties. At the time, five dominant realtors specialized in selling HUD REOs. I initially started working with one of the top brokers selling REOs, and within a year all five HUD REO brokers started using me."

"The HOC director in San Diego, Danny Mendez, was a huge advocate for FHA 203(k) financing and offered HUD REOs that needed repairs to be sold first to owner-occupied home buyers with FHA 203(k) financing. At first, I refused to do the FHA 203(k). Then, the five realtors got together and told me if I did not start doing FHA 203(k)s on their properties that required

a 203(k), then they would have to find another lender to give all their business to."

"At the time, I was doing between 5-10 HUD REOs a month and risked losing all that business, so I reluctantly started doing FHA 203(k)s. Several months later, I became well known in San Diego for being a specialist in the FHA 203(k). It got to the point where I have referred 203(k) loans from a lot of realtors and from other lenders who did not want to do the loans. My experience ranges from originating renovation loans to managing the #1 market share FHA 203(k) lender in the nation for two companies."

Ron B.

"I began my mortgage career in the broker world and during a time when things were prosperous and somewhat easy. I dabbled in a few renovation mortgages in my early years, but honestly, they were really tough to do without having been trained on them and did them very rarely. Then came the great mortgage crash, a lot of foreclosures and short sales, and a whole lot of 'bruised inventory'."

"The realtors in my market were clamoring for help to get people financed on these homes that did not meet condition requirements for regular mortgage products. I decided to dive in fully and commit myself to meeting this need in the market. My

first move was going to Wells Fargo which was by far the largest renovation lender at the time and who offered great training."

"Despite the need for these products, it was tough at the start because many in the realtor community had a bad opinion of these loans. I hit the street with excitement, only to often hear 'those loans are so hard', 'those never close on time, 'I had a horrible experience on one of those, and many more objections. I made sure to learn the process and to do these loans well, and slowly start changing those perceptions. Within a couple of years, I became one of the top renovation mortgage producers in the nation."

"Here I am years later, and still known in my market as the go-to person for all things renovation lending. I even worked with my local municipalities to create a unique pilot program allowing down payment assistance with FHA 203(k) loans, which has been an amazing success. Over the years, I have done hundreds of renovation mortgages and quite a few were 'rescue deals' where a deal was not going as well as it should somewhere else, and it just reinforced to me the importance of choosing an experienced renovation loan officer to guide the process."

"I love specializing in these loans because they let me do things others cannot do and solve problems others cannot solve, and I have seen many people's lives changed by the power of these unique products. I look forward to many more years of serving others with this knowledge, and if you are reading this

book and exploring these opportunities for yourself, I hope you also can look back one day and reflect on your own renovation success story."

Dustin S.

"When I first got into the business, I was told by my mentor and trainer that to have longevity, you need to have a niche; something you are so good at that the clients will be drawn to you like a magnet, allowing you to build a great career as a mortgage professional. What started out being a strategy to get business, over time turned into a passion and sense of fulfillment by witnessing all the good that renovation lending can do for a community."

"I picked renovation lending all those years ago because every loan officer I talked to said to run from that type of loan, and that intrigued me. That made me want to learn it even more. The more loans I closed, the more I realized that by educating realtors (and new and repeat homebuyers), the benefits of what a renovation loan can do would become apparent."

"These benefits included the ability to purchase and renovate a home with one loan and build equity; revitalizing their community one home at a time by bringing values up, renovating aged housing stock, and building wealth for themselves, for the agents, and their clients; and creating

economic activity through the purchase of materials and labor from contractors."

"These loans are a win/win/win for all stakeholders involved. Over time, I realized this, and that became more of the driving factor vs. a career strategy for longevity in the mortgage business. In the process, not only was I able to help renovate communities, but I also was able to renovate myself into the trusted advisor I am today for my clients, agents, and communities in which I serve as a whole. Renovation lending has been good to me, and it feels good to help give something back and make a difference."

Midge V.

"I fell into renovation lending quite by accident, much like I fell into the mortgage business. I had been a regular loan officer for years. We had a renovation specialist in our office, and I was happy to hand them off to someone who knew what they were doing because they were so complex."

"The renovation specialist eventually transferred, and my office needed an in-house reno specialist. My manager approached me and asked if I would be interested in becoming certified to be the new renovation specialist in the office. I already handled more complex transactions for first-time home buyers, bond programs, DAPS, grants, and affordable housing units, so I figured 'Why not?' I like HGTV, so this seemed like a perfect

fit. I drove to Boston for training and came back three days later as a certified renovation specialist."

"I love renovation financing because every client has different needs. Some just need to update. Others are customizing a home to make it ADA accessible for someone with a disability. Some are passionate about restoring an old historic home to its former glory. Sometimes it's just an update of the original style when the home was built—think 1970s paneling and shag carpet."

"Still, it's always interesting and I feel like I am truly part of making the dream of homeownership, but also the vision, a reality. I like to think I'm helping people create spaces to celebrate new babies, birthdays, holidays, and family events in the home that they created."

"Initially, we were permitted to write both renovation loans and non-renovation loans. Eventually, the company I worked for went to a model where you were either a dedicated renovation specialist or not. I had to decide to focus on just renovation or go back to being a regular loan officer. I decided to jump into renovation lending with both feet! And I haven't looked back."

Finding Solutions For The Real Estate Market

The road to the School of Hard Knocks was paved with expensive tuition for me. I was working two part-time jobs just to make payroll and relinquishing all the money out of my 401(k) just to keep up with everything. I tried hard to save those properties when I should have just let them go.

In the end, that's what I had to do. I had to let them go with all the time and money I had put into them. I had nothing left to pay, equity to strip, or a way to get out of the houses I had at the time. I'd just gotten married, and my wife had purchased a home that we moved into. The real estate market was hot when we were engaged, and I was making the most money I had in my life at the time.

Almost overnight after we got married, my wife was making three times as much as me as a nurse, whereas I was earning more than double what she was making a year before. Still, it was a very debilitating time in the early years of our marriage, and I had to find a way to help support the family. So, I rolled up my sleeves doing bartending and other odd jobs to keep up.

I then found that I couldn't make my mortgage brokerage work anymore. I went to work for a large bank instead. While I was there, I discovered a product that no one else wanted to work on. Any time I asked about it, other loan officers said: "Why would you want to do the reputation-killer loan?" All the homes for sale in the State of Florida were riddled with problems caused by being empty and closed up or weathered and left to the elements as the financial meltdown happened. No one was taking care of their property.

No one wanted to upgrade their home, either, as they thought, why put more money into an asset that had already dropped in value? Because of this, short sales and bank-owned properties arose. That market only allowed for "as is" homes to buy like a foreclosure. The banks had a bank-owned property for sale, but no one wanted to deal with them because the loan process was complicated.

I had a lot of experience doing work on homes, and I took the one loan that no one else wanted to do. I rolled up my sleeves and started to work on it. It was a renovation loan where you could buy a home with a small down payment and borrow not only the purchase price but also the renovation proceeds to fix the house up and make it turnkey ready.

Nobody knew how to put the contract together, go through due diligence inspections, get contractor bids, explain the process of how contractors were going to get paid, complete all the paperwork, get an appraisal, and close the deal. At the time, neither did I, but boy did I make a lot of discoveries along the way. It was an uphill grind to convince realtors, banks, and even customers that the loan process existed.

I finally connected the dots, and so I learned a few valuable lessons. I learned to look at the bigger picture. Instead of buying homes willy-nilly and hoping the equity situation would just take care of itself, I learned to question the cost it would take to get the house into a good state of repair and find out the future value of the home. With my process, you can learn those things and offer a good mortgage on the home. This would be a stable loan for people who want to either buy and hold property to make passive income or customize a house to make it their own.

In losing everything, I took a step back and learned how to approach the problems presented by house hacking distressed homes differently. I found solutions by working out how to use renovation loans to secure the property that seems otherwise out of reach, or too much trouble to bother with. These days, I share what I've learned with people like you so that you can make your real estate dreams come true.

I created teams of renovation loan officers and trained them to rise to the top production levels in the company. We made a system to make the complicated process digestible so anyone could apply these principles. I even took this information and put together seminars and three-hour continuing education training for realtors to break through the knowledge barrier on these products to get better market adoption. This was a grassroots campaign.

Jennifer S.

"I tell anyone who'll listen to me about mistakes I've made in buying and selling houses that need to be fixed. I wish everyone knew about the renovation loan option, as the people in my world don't have a lot of money, and they don't hear about the options available to them. My very best experience in buying a house was with a renovation loan and finding a good company to do the rehab. It works out that they take a house that wouldn't pass inspection, renovate it before you can move in, and give you a fixed house!"

"The loan funds being released to the reno company are contingent on the house passing inspection, so you know they will get that job done. It was a huge turning point for me. I don't have a lot of money, and being able to buy a foreclosed home, or distressed property at a lower price, and then be able to finance renovation costs into the loan was a game-changer for me and allowed me the opportunity to buy a home. I was able to build equity through the renovations, which was a big plus. I'd recommend this type of financing to anyone."

CHAPTER 1: INTRODUCTION

"A dream written down with a date becomes a goal. A goal broken down into steps becomes a plan. A plan, backed by action, makes your dreams come true."
~ Greg Reid

How House Hacking Has Changed My Life

I learned to house hack the hard way. I certainly put my share of hard work into the process. I wish I had a mentor, but I didn't—I had to figure it out all by myself. That was tough. Even being in the mortgage business and getting a real estate license wasn't enough of an education to prepare me for the challenges involved with rehabs and cultivating real estate deals. Nobody teaches you this in college. That's why I want to share my knowledge in this business with you in this book. This is the most responsible way I know to invest. I believe this method has the lowest risk for anyone looking to find a better way to buy a home or invest in real estate.

Financial freedom is the goal of house hacking. That means owning enough equity properties or cash flow properties to allow you to replace the income that you otherwise must work for every month. House hacking has given me a way to make money passively, as well as places to go when I travel with the family. There is also the potential for equity growth.

When I got into house hacking, I learned a niche that I love. Before I found renovation, I wasn't in love with my career, but I loved real estate. After discovering renovation loans and learning all you could do with them, I knew I was on the right track. I was on my way to becoming a house hacker when I emerged from the crash in 2008, buying my first house with cash, fixing that up, and rolling it over into more properties that I could fix, rent, and sell.

At the time, my credit was so bad that I had to use cash but still managed to figure out what I could do on a much smaller scale than today. Initially, the intent of buying that first property when I was "reborn" was to pay for my new baby daughter's pre-paid college. And it did for about a decade. I had that property which I purchase for $4, 700 in 2009. and collected $575 a month, and later sold it for $36,000. Nowadays, I am in full-fledged house hacking mode and enjoying every minute. With this book, I'm hoping to show how you, too, can benefit from renovation loans to make your real estate dreams come true.

Erin S. was working on becoming independently wealthy when I met her. She had already bought the first home with a down payment assistance program a few years earlier. Erin and her spouse were looking for something different in this purchase, though. She had read and followed *Rich Dad Poor Dad* readings and wanted to buy a home she could live in with her wife, Char, and cash flow it with other units to cover their cost of living.

They wound up finding a foreclosure on a quadplex at the beach and lived in one of the units while renting the other three out as vacation units. It needed a lot of repairs, so we were able to use a renovation program to finance the purchase and renovation with only 3.5 percent down on the total acquisition price. After the first year, they not only were net zero on their monthly outlay of cash, but they were also making several thousand dollars a month.

Eventually, they found a bigger home with two auxiliary dwelling units and a duplex on almost two acres a few years later. They had saved up some cash and were prepared to rent out the unit they were vacating to move into the next home. This was an auction property, and when they won the bid, they had to close with a loan because they didn't have all the cash. Again, here they took advantage of the renovation loan program and financed both the purchase and renovation costs.

Erin and Char are still enjoying this spacious home. They have been able to rent some of the other units, and have family stay in a few of them. They are covering their living expenses and don't have to work, but they still choose to do so. They even found a second home in the mountains that they are currently renovating and may rent it out in the future when they aren't there. They effectively built a real estate empire in five years. Would you take on some work and effort to be financially independent in five years?

What Is House Hacking?

I use the term "house hacker" to cover a range of possibilities. Technically speaking, a house hacker is someone who wants to buy a home for primary use and has the option to offset the cost of ownership by generating rental income, either by an auxiliary dwelling unit or multifamily unit.

However, you don't have to rent out your home to be a house hacker. A house hacker is someone interested in buying distressed property and fixing it up to be liveable and can go anywhere from there. If you're interested in becoming a landlord or selling your newly renovated house to generate income, then house hacking is for you.

However, you can also use house hacking to renovate that dream home you see in distressed property and make it your own. A good friend once told me: "Shavings are savings". If you like buying at the "scratch and dent store" for savings, why wouldn't you do that for real estate?

After reading this book, whether you want to engage my company's services to help you with house hacking, or you want to go it on your own, a house hacker can you be (*in the voice of Yoda*).

What Is A Distressed Home?

There are a couple of definitions of a distressed home. An appraiser would tell you that a distressed home is one belonging to someone who has a financial difficulty like a foreclosure, imminent foreclosure, late payments, short sale, or default. However, the general public would expand this definition to include homes that have less-than-desirable features. I'm not just talking about boarded-up windows, but also things like popcorn ceilings and 1970s floor plans. A lot of modern buyers consider old-fashioned layouts a problem. They want something open plan and modern, and this requires a major renovation. Wallpaper with border, phones in the toilet closet, formica countertops, and less-than-sufficient lighting are also dead giveaways that you may have a dated home.

Then there are a host of other problems that we see in distressed homes, like mold, wood rot, outdated air conditioning or roofs, and poor electrical or plumbing systems. These issues can prevent you from getting insurance on your home for closing if you have a mortgage. Unless you're dealing with cash or a renovation loan, these houses can be simply out of reach for the average home buyer. These loan programs allow you to close with different types of insurance not offered with a traditional purchase.

Sometimes, sellers are unwilling to do repairs. Listings are marketed as-is, meaning that you must buy the house as it sits. What if you have a case of wood rot or infestation? Or, what if there is a health, livability, or safety issue with the home? If you don't have a renovation loan, things can be tricky. However, if you're financing your renovation through an FHA conventional or VA renovation loan (such as we will discuss later in this book), you can make a plan to deal with these problems, which the lender agrees with to close on that house. Then, you can deal with the renovations after closing.

Another meaningful loan we did was for a single woman named Charity, who bought a duplex in downtown San Diego. At the time, downtown San Diego was a distressed area. Charity was barely qualified for the mortgage, but we were able to secure her financing and she completely renovated the duplex. A year later, San Diego passed legislation and secured funding to create a downtown redevelopment zone, and months later the San Diego Padres secured the purchase of a large piece of land downtown to build Petco Park.

As a result of the redevelopment of downtown San Diego, Charity's duplex more than quadrupled in value. I was walking in downtown San Diego with my daughter, and Charity yelled my name and came running up to me. She gave me a big hug and explained that she was now married to the love of her life. She was expecting her first child, and she told me she had sold the duplex, netting over $1 million, and bought her dream home near Del Mar. Her life was changed by doing the FHA 203(k) on that duplex. It is very common for my client's homes to be valued at more than their investment into the home, but this was a special case of buying a home at the right time in the right place.

Meeting Market Needs

These days, it's hard to find the perfect home, and some factors make home-buying more difficult. For example, for prospective buyers who might be looking to renovate, lending requirements have become more stringent, equity lending is sparse, you're competing with cash buyers in the market, the appraisal process is strict, complex and credit cards are not as available.

Furthermore, many houses on the market are distressed in one way or another. Many are as-is listings, bank foreclosures, in need of repair, or under other limitations. Eighty percent of U.S. homes are now 20 years or older (the median age is 37 years), and often in need of renovation. It's not as easy as simply picking one house out of the listings when you are shopping for a new home.

If you're ready to put a little time into it, however, there's plenty of opportunity on the market, and it can come within your reach with the appropriate renovation loan. We can help you to select the loan product that is right for you, and devise and work through a step-by-step plan to make that opportunity property into your dream home.

This is a single primary mortgage solution that allows you to access the full construction and acquisition costs into one loan with one down payment using a future value appraisal. Because of the nature of these loans, they offer a lot more sustainable solutions than more exotic loans you will find with much more stringent guidelines.

Advantages Of Buying Distressed Homes

There are several advantages to buying distressed homes. There's less competition in the market since such homes intimidate many buyers. When you see a finished home these days, multiple offers seem imminent. Finding homes that have fewer buyers can help expand real estate options. Renovation lending is also known as a "reverse BRRR investor model" (I'll talk more about BRRR in the final chapters). My process allows you to lock in the home for a price, and do all your due diligence (inspections, contractors' estimates, and appraisals) to validate how things will work before closing on that home.

Finally, there's nothing like being able to personalize a property. You can take a distressed home, which is not exactly what you want, and turn it into a dream home. We will then validate all those repairs *before* closing and before renovations to ensure that the value holds. The best part is that you can roll all of that into one loan upfront without having to spend your cash as other methods require.

How We Can Help

By using the concepts outlined in this book, you can know what the costs are upfront, and you can have one down payment, one monthly payment, and a known value for the home after repairs are finished. You can include the financing for all the materials, labor, and appliances inside your mortgage.

Our methods are relatively foolproof. If the market goes down or interest rates go up, you will have a known payment at a much lower rate than you can get on a credit card or other consumer debt, or with taking "hard money" alternatives. This method will allow you to rent and debt service the house if the market turns so you don't lose it!

Before closing, you will get an appraisal of the home's future value. This helps you not to overspend on the house. If you buy a home traditionally and start doing improvements, there is more potential to over-improving it for the area it is in. If the house doesn't appraise satisfactorily, you can revise the scope of work, drop the house altogether, or renegotiate the purchase price with the seller.

We're your partner in this process. We can help you have a lot more power as a consumer to make sure you're making a good safe bet before you close. I'll describe later how we control the cash for renovation funds and have third-party inspections to protect you from contractors and the renovation process.

Most of our solutions provide a pathway to pay the mortgage payments within the loan during construction, so you don't have to live on a construction site. You can have the mortgage payments abated while major construction work is done, so you can stay where you currently live and not struggle to make two housing payments.

I've been doing renovation lending since 2008, and I've completed and managed over 1,000 closings for renovation loans, so my organization has a lot of experience in this area. Many times, we see a broker or other lender that has little experience with these loans get knee-deep and flounder in the transaction. This is typically when we are called to come in and save the deal. Usually, this happens because of a lack of experience with these loans.

There are a lot of great lenders out there, but most of them are general practitioners. You wouldn't want to go see a podiatrist for a brain clot, so it makes sense you'd want to talk to someone that has had practice treating patients with your problem. We have several simple upfront steps in place to smooth the process and ensure success. For example, I'll only work with a company that services the loans and draws *after* closing. Otherwise, it can be tough to pay the contractor, leading to nightmares for the customer even after we close the deal.

There are very few lenders willing to tackle this space in housing because it's not an automated, simple process like conventional products can be. As a result of new mortgage lending rules in the last decade, loan officers cannot make a higher commission, the process takes a lot of work, and the likelihood of closing these loans can be lower than in regular loans (for most loan officers, at least).

That doesn't apply to us. Some lenders prefer to limit what repairs they will allow, whereas we can cover most repairs with the processes we'll be outlining in this book. All lenders are not equal, and it is vital to use a good loan company with an experienced renovation loan officer that offers a full line of renovation products and will service the renovation draw.

We can help you identify the home, assist you and your agent to go under contract with the home, get inspections, review the inspections with the contractor, and get a contractor's bid before receiving the appraisal for the home. Just like a cash investor, you can make an "as-is" purchase offer on the home to get under contract.

Then, we help with the process of doing inspections. Only after having the inspections and knowing everything that's wrong with the house, though, do we get the contractors to make a full estimate. Once we have the bid, we secure the appraisal that drives the process for closing. The appraisal process gives us the future value of the home after the repairs are done. Then, we can get the loan underwritten and closed. After closing, we can start releasing the funds for the renovation process to begin.

There are three main programs involved: the FHA 203(k), the VA renovation, and the homestyle renovation loans. To help you choose the one that's right for you, we will go over each of these programs in detail later in this book. With these programs, you can identify properties that can use some improvement, and buy them often at a discount. Then, we'll use our step-by-step process to renovate them to your preference.

Beyond Basic House Hacking

For those that are interested, this book also goes beyond the purchase of the home and talks about marketing your distressed property. I call this process "advanced house hacking."

Once you have a property, you may want to live in it, rent it out, or sell it. In this book, I discuss marketing techniques for agents who are interested in selling distressed homes. I'll outline the concepts of the instant equity involved in a ready-to-go home, and the sweat equity earned through renovation.

In advanced house hacking, we'll talk about various tools that can earn you more equity for your home. Second homes and short-term vacation rentals made more popular by VRBO and Airbnb are a way to generate income from your rehabbed properties. We'll also discuss BRRR (buy, rehabilitate, rent, and refinance). (Thank you, Robert Kaisekis!) We'll talk about the advantages and disadvantages of this technique, and why doing a renovation loan is a better option.

I'll also talk about 1031 exchanges, which are used to invest one home's profits into the next home without having to pay taxes right away.

Who Should Read This Book?

This book is a useful resource for anybody curious about renovation loans, or anyone who is looking to buy real estate using these products with their customers and wants success in this space.

I know that there are many claims out there on methods of buying real estate. I can't guarantee that you will agree this is the best way to do it, but I can say that this is my system, which has made me and my customers a lot of money. So, you should definitely consult a CPA or lawyer, but if you like what you read, I hope it's helpful to you because it certainly has helped me. I'll tell you about some of my customers' successes on the way, too, and even some of my failures.

If you're not scared away by now, I invite you to dig into this book. If you find something interesting in it and want to talk about it, send me your questions at thehousehackingbook@gmail.com or thehousehackingbook.com. We're here for you through the process, and hope you enjoy learning how to house hack!

CHAPTER 2: THE MODERN HOUSING MARKET

"As we evolve, our homes should too."
~ Suzanne Tucker Interiors

The modern housing market is a conundrum. People have updated their ideas about what they want in a home, but the homes available for sale are older and do not necessarily reflect current trends. Many older homes present problems in terms of layout, efficiency, and wear and tear. While the renovation isn't for everyone, it represents a great solution to the problems presented by older homes, and it's an invigorating challenge for those who are willing to take it on.

The Modern Market: A Renovation Market

Today's consumers are often looking for something with at least three bedrooms and two baths. They likely want a home office, and maybe bonus rooms like a kids' playroom. With the aging baby boomers, multigenerational housing is often sought after. An in-law solution, such as a suite, can be a valuable option. Most buyers are looking for an open plan, modern layout with up-to-date fixtures and appliances.

People like warm areas to gather in, such as a kitchen and living room that flow together in one large welcoming space. Most people prefer solid surface floors rather than carpets, solid color cabinets rather than wood or veneer, quartz or other durable, higher-end countertops, and great lighting.

Consumers are also interested in efficiency. They want low-maintenance options and low operating costs, so the home must be energy efficient, with quality insulation and efficient heating and cooling systems. Increasingly, consumers are interested in up-to-date solar or other energy-efficient upgrades. House hacking reduces our carbon footprint by getting more use of the space you are acquiring. That's a side benefit to what we do.

The hard truth in housing these days is that the house people are often looking for simply does not exist in the area. The average age of houses in the United States is 37 years. If you think about it, that means most houses on the market are basically outdated for today's needs. As I write this, I'm approaching 41. I've never considered myself "old", but when you think of a home built in the 1980s, there could be a lot of systems within the house approaching their economic end.

What was in vogue 30 or 40 years ago? A lot of older homes on the market these days are two bedrooms and one bath. Wallpaper, Formica countertops, popcorn ceilings, carpets, several closed-in rooms, and boxed-off kitchens were all the rage. Open plan layouts were not a fashion in the 1980s.

Few buyers these days want these things. People aren't necessarily looking for a huge home, but they do want functional space. They want rooms that can be used in a multifunctional manner. The kitchen and living areas have become a gathering space for social time. With many more people working from home these days, the extra bedroom has become a guest room/office (if there isn't already a dedicated home office). People expect their homes to keep up with a busy modern lifestyle.

If it's not an outdated floor plan, it could be something else that makes homes for sale less than desirable. Older houses might have issues with mold or rot; they might need new air conditioning or insulation, a new roof, or updated plumbing and electrical systems. Sometimes, they even have trouble with structural or foundation issues. Much of the time, sellers list these houses "as-is", meaning that they will be sold as they are, imperfections and all. It's up to the buyer to repair the home.

With all these problems, older homes aren't necessarily ideal, but they're often located in desirable neighborhoods that are safe, closer to downtown or shopping areas, or family friendly. They may be priced well, but less than ideal for the buyer and their family. That's where renovations come into play. With a renovation loan, these houses can be updated and made into perfect homes once again: modern and ideally located.

A Better Way To Tackle Renovations

Currently, there's a very limited inventory of desirable, modern, move-in-ready homes on the market. Homes with modern standards sell quickly, often at premium prices. These houses usually become the subject of multiple offers and bidding wars because everyone wants them. This drives the prices up.

The homes that are not being sold under a flurry of multiple offers are the ones that need a bit of renovation and TLC. These houses abound, and people often buy them assuming that they can put in the work overtime. However, this can be a stressful trap to fall into. Many times, the home may be in such a poor condition that a normal loan won't allow for its purchase.

After closing on the property, people who want to do the renovations over time can find that they are financially stretched and stressed while living in a construction zone. They get into credit card debt, and they wind up getting equity lines and second mortgages. It's difficult to get junior loans on a house right after closing, especially if the home is in disrepair (in the middle of construction). There is a stress of trying to live in a home while sections of it are under renovation.

Right before I got married, I lived in a house I was trying to rehab the wrong way, and my wife refused to get married until I had a working kitchen in the house. Later when we were married, and the air conditioner wouldn't work for a few days, she moved in with her parents until I could get it working. These problems can inflame issues in the marriage!

Unfortunately, these examples are all too common. My friend owns a home that he partially renovated before he and his family moved in. Today, the hardwood floors they should have installed remain carpeted because…life.

A lack of proper planning can lead some people to over-renovate the house or underestimate what they need to get it up and running. Most assume that their jewel of a home is worth more than typical homes in the area, and they are later surprised they cannot sell the house for as much as they put into it.

When undertaken at the time of purchase, renovation loans provide an answer to these problems. The process of doing a renovation loan will validate that you are making a wise investment before you do the improvements, so you don't over-improve the house. Your costs for renovations and the value of the house post-renovation will be known, so you can know right away if it will appraise at an appropriate value for the area, it's located. Therefore, you will be able to get your money back if you decide to sell the house.

If you aren't happy—if the house does not appraise to your liking—you can revise the scope of work, drop the house altogether, or renegotiate the purchase price with the seller. More importantly, we have the answers to costs to make sure you have enough funds for closing and an additional amount called contingency funds (which we will discuss later), just in case the scope of work needs to change, or it costs more than originally anticipated.

Doing a renovation loan allows you to have a manageable payment schedule, rather than having to deal with credit card debt and second mortgages. You'll know what the costs are upfront with one down payment and one monthly payment. The mortgage, including the renovation loan, will have manageable payments at a good conforming interest rate, which will protect you if the market goes up and interest rates go up.

Perhaps, most importantly, the renovations can all be done upfront, before you move into the house, so you don't have to live in a construction zone and deal with all the stress that causes. As well, you can start enjoying the improvements right away. You'll be able to live in your personalized dream home immediately, not just wish for it year after year as you do one small renovation at a time.

The Renovation-Oriented Consumer

Simply put, it is often impossible to find the home of your dreams in the area you desire. If you want that dream home in the right area, renovations will most likely be required, and this calls for a change in outlook on the part of the consumer. Renovations are not for everyone, but for more and more people, they are a viable option to get the home they want in the area they want, all at a good price.

Luckily, many modern home buyers are changing their outlook and expectations in ways that help meet the demands of the modern house market. Many of today's consumers who turn to renovation tend to be courageous, industrious, resourceful, and creative. They have the moxie to attack the challenge and see it through, along with a remarkable vision for the potential of their new home. Frequently, they have a strong desire for something better than the cookie-cutter experience, and the willingness to see past the home's current state to transform a project into reality. If this sounds like you, then you may find success with renovation lending.

Dan D. used these same principles at the early age of 20. At the time, he was working at a pizza shop and was able to buy a modest foreclosure at the beach that needed much work. Even though the neighborhood was great, the house needed a lot of love. That allowed Dan to get it at a reduced price.

Ten years later, he is on his third property acquisition. Specifically, he acquired two investment properties, but he still lives in the original house we helped him buy. He has added a swimming pool and refinanced to lower rates since then. Dan also has managed to start his own pizzeria, and I can personally attest that he has the best Philly pizza and wings in town. Dan was truly an ambitious client in his work and personal investments. Know that he did his real estate plan and laid the path over time. He didn't create it all in one night. However, he has amassed a great source of passive income and equity in the short time he committed to the process.

Most people who are successful with renovation loans and house hacking are investment oriented. Your primary home is, of course, for your initial intent and use. Still, you will typically need to think outside the box to find a better-than-average purchase. I'm asking you to keep an open mind here and not look at a house merely as a home. Rather, think of it as a savings bank, and strive to make home purchases as part of a long-term, well-thought-out strategic plan.

I know that doesn't sound super-sexy, but consider this: Doesn't a house that can have enough equity to pay for its own pool sound intriguing? If the market dips, you want to have equity and appreciation in your home to draw upon or help ease out curves in the market. If you need to sell, borrow, or transfer equity to another investment, you always want an exit strategy. Hope is not a plan to make money in real estate (nor is it in most facets of life). It takes strategic planning and time, along with money and finances.

A wide variety of people have used our services to get help with renovation lending, and so we have many success stories to illustrate the benefits of our process. Check out some more of our stories, as well as a few other stories I will share about other top-performing renovation lenders that have helped with input on this book and some of their clients' top successes. Do any of these people sound like you? We'd love to hear from you!

A young couple wanted a home that they could personalize to meet the needs of the lady's disability that was incurred after a stroke. None of the homes they looked at had the accommodations necessary for her wheelchair, so we helped them find a foreclosure. With the money they saved, they were able to widen doorways, lower countertops, and improve the bathrooms. Once they had customized the home, they still made equity.

We have helped first-time home buyers leverage into houses that needed a ton of TLC using a renovation loan. The renovation created enough equity to eliminate mortgage insurance within a year of purchase.

We have helped countless clients buy homes that were considered "cash only" or "as is." These homes would have been out of reach or impossible to finance without a renovation loan. We've also helped people finance "uninsurable" homes with these products.

House hacking is a way to invest money in homes and see returns. We've helped investors buy homes that they intended to keep without having to use hard money. They buy, renovate, and keep the loan on the house so they can rent it out, thus earning money on their properties.

Renovation: A Solution To The Modern Housing Market

The modern housing market is tough. There are a lot of "fixer-uppers" out there, and few ready-to-move-in homes. Those that exist are generally offered at premium prices. It's important to know, though, that renovation lending can change a fixer-upper into a modern dream home, or an investment opportunity. It takes a little courage and a lot of vision, but renovation is a way to create something new and special in desirable places to live, where these homes didn't exist before.

You can transform your home from the worst to the best on the block. The modern renovation-oriented consumer, armed with a little imagination and a lot of resourcefulness, is up for the challenge, and we have helped many people make their dreams into reality. So, I encourage you to find a location and then look for the opportunity in that location, rather than a "perfect home".

Martin S. was a single dad living at the beach with four young boys. He was trying to find a place in a nicer neighborhood to raise his kids. One of his sons had special needs and they wanted to be close to his friends' schools and support network, but what he was looking for wasn't out there. He then found a bright-orange four-bedroom house that needed a major overhaul and was in foreclosure.

Martin was able to find his family a place that needed significant improvement, get it for pennies on the dollar, and fix it up into a nice home. Importantly, he got a place in a good neighborhood for his kids to grow up. As well, he now has a home he can afford and has made a significant equity play. He has more equity than he could have had at the same price in a worse neighborhood, away from his support system and certainly without the equity cushion.

CHAPTER 3: HOUSE HACKING: A SOLUTION TO CURRENT MARKET NEEDS

"Diligence is the beginning of brilliance."
~ Indonesian Proverb

The best news I haven't shared yet is that you don't have to go at this all alone. I threw out some new concepts in the previous chapters that may have you thinking this is too much for a person with little purchase experience. The current market is a tough one for new home buyers, but there are solutions. We've explored this market thoroughly, and we've learned some lessons that we can pass on to you, the prospective buyer, about why renovation lending is a great option for today's market.

We've also talked about how to begin your journey by preparing what you will need. The first step in getting into real estate is to assemble a good team that can help you start putting a plan together with a diligent mindset.

Why Renovation Lending?

With almost any market, you have a certain number of people in the buyer pool for homes, no matter what the price range is—it could be a one hundred thousand dollar or a million-dollar home. For an uncomplicated, new build or no-renovation needed home, you will always be competing with more buyers. The sheer competition will drive sale prices up and make it harder to buy the dream home you are looking for.

However, things can get more complicated quickly. For example, let's say that the house needs renovations, is physically distressed, or it's a short sale, under probate, or a foreclosure. In those cases—and especially if the house has cosmetic challenges or requires major repairs—the number of people you are competing with for that house falls. Buying in the renovation market can make it easier to get the home you desire because you don't have to compete with so many other people to get it.

If you can get a good purchase price on a home that needs some repairs and acquire repairs for an improved future value, then you're going to make some money in the process. Using a renovation plan for a home allows you to lock it in for a price and to do your due diligence with inspectors and contractors before closing. You can personalize and customize that home to your own needs, thus adding value to that house.

Suzannah was retiring to a historic district and wanted to buy another house there as a second home. It was her dream to retire to Amelia Island, and she knew had found the perfect opportunity. Even though the real estate market was red hot, there was one home that had a structural issue and had been on the market for quite some time. There were some leveling issues with the structure of the house, which was on the home disclosure and was visible upon entry.

With a renovation loan, she was able to do a cosmetic renovation and fix the structural issues as well. The contractor had warranty guarantees on the structural repair and was able to fix the house in the process. When the appraisal came back, it validated our pre-renovation plan. We had believed that adding the repairs would make the house worth a lot more than her total acquisition. It made perfect sense to move forward with it.

People argue that buying a brand-new home means you don't have to do any maintenance on the house, but in reality, you're just putting that maintenance off. The years go by and, before you know it, you need a new roof. No matter how you look at it, eventually, you are going to have to make room in your budget for repairs if you own real estate. Why not take an older home and ensure that you have the big stuff done and warrantied right up front so you can make a reasonable budget?

With a renovation, you can make that old home like new from the start. You can make it your own, with all the personalized details that you want. *You don't have to settle for anything.* After all, when you choose options on a new home, all you are doing is improving it beyond the builder's standards and financing it over 30 years…just like a renovation loan.

A renovation plan allows you to add all your renovations onto your mortgage, rather than using a credit card or line of credit. You can possibly write off the mortgage interest, and it will be at a lower rate than credit, especially if it is spread out over several years like a 30-year mortgage. Credit cards and lines of credit can have high-interest rates that can really eat up your profits and drive down the amount of money you are keeping in your pocket.

If you are an investor, high-interest credit can ruin your ability to win in the marketplace. Investors often use hard money to renovate their homes, which is an expensive choice when there are other options available. Usually, they use the BRRRR (buy, renovate, rent, refinance, and repeat) method, which we will talk about more in later chapters. This is a good old-school strategy, but it's just that: "old school." We can consolidate those steps in the method we will lay out for you.

The BRRR approach involves buying a home, spending money on renovations, and then trying to do a cash-out refinancing. It is usually a hard money loan with higher interest rates for the first mortgage and two sets of closing costs. When you refinance, you are supposed to take a cash-out and get the money back you spent on renovation or equity strip. To me, it just doesn't make sense when you can get all the financing up front with a renovation loan, do everything, and pay a lower rate of interest.

I recommend a buy-and-hold strategy, rather than flipping the house or equity stripping. This allows you to cash flow that property in any market. If the market were to crash, then you would be insulated with a mortgage, while you rent out the property to make your mortgage payments. Believe me, I know! If I had done that in the last crash, I would still have those properties, and I would cautiously estimate my net worth would be at least several million higher.

However, my misstep in the late 2000s—my hard landing, if you will—is your benefit.

A renovation loan allows you to include the finances for all the materials, labor, and appliances inside your mortgage with one monthly payment. You may have tax deductibility, and it will definitely be at a lower rate than credit cards. Before you close, right up front, you will get an appraisal for the home's future value.

Again, we will not typically want to know the as-is value or condition of the house. We will be able to see the home's future value all fixed up, unlike when you buy a home and put in repairs and upgrades gradually over time. You will ensure that you are not over-or under-improving the home for the area you are purchasing. The strategy here is if you had to sell, you will want to get at least the money back out of the house that you put into it. Don't forget that there are closing costs and commissions when you sell, so plan for buffers for these costs as well.

All of these are excellent reasons to consider a renovation loan, and in the following chapters, we will look at the different products available. If, after reading this, you've decided to take on a renovation and house hack your way to home ownership, then it is time to start looking at how to go about doing so.

Things To Think About Before Hunting For A House

Over the years, I have made every mistake in the book. Some of my failures are probably the best examples of what not to do when it comes to renovation hacks. I have experimented with every way of buying and renovating houses, and I have learned a few tips about how to do it successfully with standard renovation loans.

I have created an outline for home buying that reduces the headaches involved in renovation and financing and maximizes your profit. This is not the only way to do it, but it is the most systematic way you can build a plan for success. Every time I deviated from it, I lost money!

Property values have been skyrocketing lately, so it seems that people have been making money no matter how they go about the process. Know that there is a more efficient way to go about it that makes your life a lot easier. You see, part of our plan is to make sure we protect profits by not spending money unnecessarily, and you must include an exit strategy.

It is *extremely* important to note that buying a home based solely on value and future equity is a poor decision. It fails to take into account the value of repairs that you are going to have to do. No one knows when a house value will reach a certain point in value until it is sold, and no one knows if the market will turn on you. You can, however, evaluate the home's value accurately based on its condition and future value from those repairs. It's important to get costs and make sure the purchase price and the costs are consistent with the future value.

Amy and Mike get stationed here in Jacksonville recently. They both wanted something that was not cookie cutter and found it hard to get a "deal" on a home. They were already approved with a local lender that did renovation loans, but they had a repair amount cap for the VA program and the bank they were working with. Their agent connected them to me to help them dream through a home that had been on the market for a while and required a ton of work to bring it up to par. A benefit of this home was that it included another lot.

They bought the home for around $100,000 with the additional lot and needed renovation of about $225,000 to bring this historic gem back to luster. Sadly, after making great friends with these clients, they were deployed again to Texas and had to sell. The good news is that since they did a great job on buying well and improving the house, they sold it for a profit in the mid $500,000s! This proves that you can find a deal in almost any market.

Your Trusted Team

Buying real estate is not a solo journey. You will need a trusted team to help you with the details of any home purchase. A trusted team will consist of real estate agents, lenders, home inspectors, contractors, real estate attorneys, insurance agents, and certified public accountants. You need someone who can give you solid legal advice, someone who can advise you on the title and curing title problems, help in creating a trust, knows market saturation and values, can help you negotiate, and is great at inspecting a home.

You also need someone to analyze the costs of repairs, someone to give financial feedback and advice, and someone to keep you in bounds with write-off deductions and square with the IRS. You need to make an appointment with these folks and interview a few of them. Find someone who you can relate with and feel like they will give you the service and attention you need to close the deal.

Ask yourself: "Do these people provide the kind of service I would seek to offer if I was in their position?" This means they are good at keeping you on task and will hold you accountable. This person should not be your best drinking buddy with a license or a relative that just got their license. I know I am going to get hate mail for saying that, but you should assemble a team based on merit in the industry. After all, this isn't personal; it's business.

All these people are very important in your real estate business. It is wise to hire them based on your comfort and the reputation of the person you are doing business with. I am blatantly telling you *not* to choose the person with the cheapest fees in any of these fields. Any one of these trades is also bound to have expenses attached to them, but these people are worth their weight in gold for the money they can make and/or save you for the experience they will provide!

Brett was a great example of an awesome partner in real estate. When Fred's tenant destroyed his house, Brett connected him to a contractor to get his home back into shape. He then introduced Fred to an attorney to recover lost rent and funds for repairs. He marketed and sold the home so Fred could move on. Brett found that the home had significant equity, and rather than just do a quick sale, referred Fred to a 1031 specialist to avoid capital gains. Brett also connected Fred to a short-term rental property that just came on the market and was able to move the funds to a new investment without having to pay taxes right away on the equity of the previous sale.

One of the mistakes many people make is involving family and friends in these roles who have little experience. You trust mom and dad. You trust friends and family that they are looking out for you. While most parents and friends want what is best for their children, they're only human; they too have biases that influence their advice.

Wouldn't you rather have someone working on your solutions that has had more at-bats? With loved ones, sometimes *their* idea of what is best for you is not *your* idea of what is best for you, and it can be hard to say "no" to them. Also, if you are relying on your trusted team of professionals, they have a myriad of experiences in helping people succeed.

You want people on your team who have as much experience as possible so that they can lend you the value of their knowledge. Again, this isn't personal.

Lessons I Have Learned: Due Diligence

Every time I have failed in real estate, I can point back to certain specific errors. One is not using my trusted team system. It may sound cliché, but when you have the right people advising you, they can see errors that you miss. They can help you foresee and work through potential future problems as well.

Or I was not doing some kind of necessary homework. For example, I was just trusting that the future value or equity of a home would bail me out of my situation. This always wound up getting me into a bad deal and was a major part of what got me and everyone else in trouble in 2008.

A lot of people buy houses based on emotion. A house makes them feel good, so they want it. Emotion is very *illogical* in real estate. You want to enjoy the place you are going to live in, but making decisions purely based on emotion can lead to pitfalls. A home is also an investment;

they are the same thing. Learn from my experience. I had to figure this out the hard way.

You need to know going into a deal what you will be spending money on before you close on that house. It's important to do your due diligence. Sometimes, you will make discoveries that cause you to not even buy the house you are contemplating. That's okay. Your trusted team is very important when you are carefully examining a home. They can carry out proper inspections, so you know what the house needs.

You also need people who know the market and have the experience to gauge future values and market saturation rates correctly. They must be able to conduct comparative market analysis to get accurate future numbers on a home before you even spend money on an appraisal. An experienced team can help you plan how to improve a house to the market standard for that particular neighborhood before you even make an offer. That helps you avoid over-or under-improvements.

John bought a home in desperation after waiting almost eight months to get into his next investment opportunity. A local broker was selling what looked like a multifamily opportunity out of his family's estate. It sat on the market for quite a while, but John was convinced that he could get it into shape. When he closed on the home after waiving contingencies and disregarding the advice his trusted network gave him, it wound up being in a lot worse shape than he thought it would be.

Then, the pandemic hit, and he couldn't get any contractors to show up. It ended up categorized as an unusable primary dwelling that needed to be demolished. It had a septic system that had to be replaced, and in desperation, he placed a manufactured home on top of it. John lost about $35,000 on that house. It was an expensive lesson that could have been 100 percent avoidable. If he had followed any of the systematic principles, we will lay out here, he would have avoided this costly mistake.

The home you are contemplating might tickle your emotions, and that's okay, but remember it is an investment. You need to know everything about that home before you consider closing an offer on it. If you have a question about anything with a house—like something that's going on with an air conditioner unit, the heating, the roof, mold issues, radon gas, or lead-based paint—then you need to have these details inspected.

Most people don't know that you can call your local municipality for the heating and electricity costs for that home before closing. Get those numbers and know what it is going to cost you before you enter a contract. If you know that there's a repair required, you will want to understand how much that repair is going to cost you. A contractor you trust can be an invaluable asset in situations like this.

Have you gotten an insurance quote yet? Sometimes, the house can present challenges on insurance. Have there been any previous claims? Do you have any items that fail inspections for your insurance requirements? Does the age of some appliance or structure (like the roof) affect your insurance? Are you in a special area where wind, sinkhole, flood, or earthquake insurance might be required? Again, part of your team will involve an insurance provider.

You need to establish how you want to take title and ownership of your property. Many people take ownership in their personal names. I do not recommend you do this…ever. There are a lot of problems that can stem from this. Instead, I highly recommend everyone consult with a real estate or estate planning lawyer to see about creating a trust for all their assets. Several investors prefer to take the title in the corporate name, but this is, in my opinion, not the right solution.

If you know all these things, you are likely to make a good investment in a home, even if there is emotion involved in your decision. Do your due diligence, have the home inspected, and know your numbers. All these steps will help ensure that you avoid financial pitfalls even before you close on that home.

I said all of this before getting qualified for financing. Sometimes, you are or aren't ready to buy a home based on the money. Getting qualified is the first step in your buying process, and you want a specialist if you are using these kinds of products. If you truly want to buy a home but aren't qualified, that still doesn't stop you from creating a plan and putting your trusted team of professionals to work today.

If anything can be a blessing from not being qualified, then consider this. If you have sat down with a lending professional, they have likely given you a pathway to correct the problem and genuine advice on how you can turn your situation around. Like a renovation plan, you can put that into action now.

If you are thinking about renovation lending for buying your dream home or even buying a home at all, then it's time to act. You wouldn't buy a stock or make a large investment without considering it, would you? Begin to assemble a trusted team to help you with your decisions and consider carefully all the steps needed to do due diligence on the homes you will be contemplating.

We will go into more detail about the process in the chapters to come, but it's never too early to prepare yourself for the endeavor of buying a home. After all, as much as a home is an emotional choice, it is also an investment. You must consider it as such from the beginning of the process.

CHAPTER 4: RENOVATION LENDING

"Renovating old homes is not about making them look new...it is about making new unnecessary."
~ Ty McBride

Renovation loans have wide applicability. They can be used for any home requiring renovation. There's always something that you can change about the house you want to buy, and with a renovation loan you can purchase with that in mind to create your dream home, in your desired neighborhood, and where it does not currently exist. The renovation loan makes this easy for everyone, including the first-time home buyer, house hacker, or even the investor.

In this chapter, we will look at some of the preconceived notions that people have about renovation lending and the truths about these notions. We will also examine the major types of renovation loans, and what you can and cannot do with each of them. This will help you get a better idea of which loan might be right for you.

Truths About Renovation Lending

You may have some existing ideas about renovation loans. Some of these will be true and some may be misconceptions. You may have found some of them online. The information you get while surfing the Net can conflict, and it may vary between lenders. There is a lot of information out there, and not all of it is accurate. Here, we'll review some of the notions that people have about renovation lending and tell some truths.

One misconception that people have about renovation lending is that you need more than one appraisal. The truth is, in renovation lending, we only care about the future value of the home when we are doing a purchase; otherwise, what we need is one appraisal of the "as-is" value and one for the future value of the home. First, we will need a bid from the contractor that includes all the repairs that will bring the home into its new condition. This way, any issues with the house that would otherwise prevent lending can be addressed after closing.

Detrimental conditions can be overlooked, based on contracted repairs that are in the contractor's report. Additionally, the appraiser can consider the value of future conditions (like a new kitchen or bath) that are going to add value to the home. This future value appraisal will get the purchase and renovations validated for the total acquisition cost of the house for the purchase amount.

Another perception of renovation loans is that there are multiple closings. Unlike a construction loan, where you are building a brand-new home and there are draws and payments based on balances and subsequent draws of funds (and where we usually need to go to a modification or a final mortgage with multiple closings), a renovation loan product allows us to close with one known payment. There is one closing, one payment, and a known rate from the date that you lock in through the life of the loan (just like a regular purchase).

Renovation loans are often said to be expensive. This is true to some extent, but not by much. They are usually from a quarter to a half percent higher than a regular loan of the same variety. Meaning, for example, if you are comparing a VA renovation to a regular VA loan or the FHA 203(k) to a regular FHA or FHA 203(b) loan. It is difficult to compare two different things, though, like a regular 30-year fixed loan versus a loan that involves the renovation and/or construction.

The difference is based on different risk grades, which are provided by government-sponsored entities that set risk-based pricing on all the loans we use, whether they be conventional or government-based. Renovation loans are higher due to a slightly higher risk. There are also additional fees, such as the appraisal fee and supplemental fees for draw servicing payments to the contractor. The difference can be as high as 1 percent, depending on how the market is behaving.

Even though it's higher due to risk factors, this higher rate gives you a completely different product. In the end, based on the total acquisition price, it gives you a better total dollar investment on what you want compared to a ready-to-go home. This will allow you, for instance, to finance a home that couldn't typically be financed any other way and, potentially, could miss out on altogether. Renovation loans allow you to do repairs, thus giving you a completely different home that you can start enjoying.

Many of our clients have refinanced after going through these loan products. A VA (Veterans Affairs) loan, for instance, is eligible for refinancing, allowing you to take advantage of your equity position. Market rates are always shifting, and you can take advantage as rates go down. Most clients experience equity.

For my FHA and conventional clients, this usually means removing mortgage insurance after renovation due to increased equity and *lower loan value*. Once repairs are done, you are able (without a prepayment penalty) to refinance to perhaps a lower rate, and potentially cancel mortgage insurance if you have gained enough equity position versus the cash you put into the original transaction.

Another preconceived notion is that you must use specific contractors or have multiple bids. Neither is a requirement, although as a consumer, it's always a good idea to have multiple bids from general contractors. I always recommend using a licensed, insured general contractor. One reason is because of their experience in scheduling and managing the subcontractors to do the work required.

For example, an experienced contractor knows to schedule the ceiling renovation before the floors, so that the ceiling-repair process doesn't destroy the newly renovated floors. This may seem like a common-sense detail, but it's surprising how often things like this are overlooked in renovations. A trusted realtor or HUD (Department of Housing and Urban Development) consultant can help you find a good general contractor. There are also several online resources to search for contractors, such as Angi (formerly known as Angie's List).

Sometimes, people want to perform all the work themselves. We do not recommend this option. The loans are more difficult to close as is and adding self-help to them will complicate the process further. If you do pursue self-help, you will have a lot of restrictions added to your draw and disbursement steps. You can certainly opt to have only one bid from a licensed general contractor of your choosing; for example, if you have a friend who is a contractor who allows you to work under their license. That is allowed under these programs.

In most states, there is a general fund for the contractor to protect you if you use a general contractor to complete the project in case something happens, and your general contractor fails in some way to do so. If you only use subcontractors, in most states, there is no general fund to protect you, and you are the only point of accountability to deliver your entire project. So, it is in the best interest of protecting your project to use a general contractor.

Finding a general contractor can be the most challenging part of a renovation loan. It is a myth that you have to choose from some pre-approved list. Online, there are a lot of contractors that offer various services (like on Angi). However, some of these people are subcontractors. We always recommend that you rely on your trusted team to source a qualified, insured general contractor for your project.

A real estate advisor or a HUD consultant can be a valuable asset for this search. A HUD consultant who is licensed as a home inspector can come to the house, look at the entire project, and give you an idea of what it will cost because they bid on these projects all day long. They are in a no-bid consultative capacity where they can give you advice and opinions on what to do, and they can make suggestions on contractors. This way, you can know what the approximate cost is right away for the repairs before you put the project out to bid.

There is one small and easily corrected exception to this rule. For VA renovation loans, there is a published list of contractors on the VA's approved list site. If your contractor is not on this list, it typically only takes about 48 hours to get a VA pin for a builder ID, which validates the contractor's insurance and other administrative details. If you do have a contractor you want to use for your VA renovation loan and they aren't on the list, we can usually have them added quite easily.

You should not get a list of contractors from your loan officer, as loan officers cannot recommend contractors. This is deemed to be a steering practice and is prohibited. Some loan officers disregard the rule from HUD and have a list of contractors they prefer to use. I think there is too much opportunity for collusion and kickbacks when referrals are passed this way to contractors, and most customers agree. You should interview your contractor to make sure they are a good fit for you, not just your lender.

Your contractor will have to agree with the method used by the lender to pay for repairs for the process to run smoothly. Sometimes, your contractor will attempt to dictate the payment process in their estimate and summary. We'll discuss this in more detail in Chapter 6.

Finally, there is a perception out there that renovation loans are extremely complicated or that they never close. Renovation loans can certainly be more complicated than standard loans, and for this reason, a lot of lenders will not take them on. However, they are not impossible. It takes a specialized back-office process and a loan officer that understands the steps and procedures to work successfully with these loans.

I have closed and managed more than a thousand in 20 years. They do require a bit more work from both your lender and your real estate agent, who must open the house more often to let in contractors and inspectors. The loan will not be ready to go until you have made decisions about what you want to do with the house and how you are going to renovate it, and you cannot make these decisions until you have estimates about the costs involved.

Once you have three things under your belt—the contractor, inspections, and a final bid—you have the hardest part of renovations tackled. Therefore, it's true that renovation loans are a bit more complicated than regular loans, but in the end, they are worth the effort.

Types Of Renovation Loans

What can and can't you do with a renovation loan? That depends on the loan you are looking at using. Let's start with a quick look at each type of loan.

The Federal Housing Authority 203(k)

This product has two types, called the Limited (sometimes referred to as Streamline) or the Consultant K. It is a one-size-fits-all primary residence program. You must intend to live in the house and may have mortgage insurance for the life of the loan. The 203(k) also allows for lower credit scores just like the regular FHA program. Typically, the down payment is as little as 3.5 percent. On HUD foreclosures, they can be as little as $100!

For the Limited version of the loan, repairs must be under $35,000 in total with the contingency reserve. You cannot have structural repairs or add square footage. You don't need a HUD consultant for this loan product, and this version of the loan does not include a payment abatement. This is the most common renovation loan.

There are many misconceptions about the renovation amounts on this loan type, as some lenders do not offer both of these products. Contrary to some information you could get from a lender stating that repairs cannot be over $35,000, may just mean you are talking to a lender that doesn't offer the product.

With Consultant K, you can finance the payments (in a payment abatement), and you don't have to live in the house while it is under construction. The HUD consultant can include the payment abatement in this case, which is a big advantage. You can also have repairs over $35,000 up to no maximum amount. This loan can apply to single-family residences, 1–4-unit residences, mixed-use properties, mobile homes, and other applications.

Luxury items (such as pools, jetted tubs, and tennis courts) are not allowed with these loans. You can repair an existing pool, but you cannot have a new one built. Irrigation systems and landscaping are not allowed, but you can do site improvements such as soil-retaining walls, drainage, and turf to prevent soil loss.

RENOVATION
QUICK REFERENCE GUIDE

	FHA 203K (STANDARD)	FHA 203K (LIMITED)	FANNIE MAE HOMESTYLE	VA RENOVATION
LOAN TYPE	Purchase or Refinance	Purchase or Refinance	Purchase or Refinance	Purchase or Refinance
MORTGAGE AMOUNT	Lower of: Total Cost (sales price + renovation) or 110% of "As completed" Appraised Value		Lower of: Total Cost (sales price + renovation) or "As completed" Appraised Value	
MAXIMUM LTV	Purchase: 96.5% of Sale price + Total Rehab No Cash Out Refinance: 97.5% of Mortgage Payoff + Total Rehab		95% for 1 — Unit Primary See Guidelines for Other Property Types	100%
RENOVATION AMOUNTS	Minimum: $5,000	Minimum: $2,000	Minimum: $5,000	LIMITED - Minimum: $0 STANDARD - Minimum: $5,000
	Max: No Max As Long As Mortgage Amounts Are Within County Guidelines For FHA Loans	Max: Up To $35,000 Total Including All Costs & Fees	Max: 75% of the As Completed Appraised Value	LIMITED – Max. Up To $35,000 Total Including All Costs Fees STANDARD – No Maximum
ALLOWABLE REPAIRS	From Complete Rehab, Including Structural Changes, New Appliances and More	Flooring to Painting Remodeling Kitchen/Bath, Appliances and More. No Major Remodeling or Structural Repairs	Repairs Must be Affixed and Add Value to the Property	Flooring to Painting Remodeling Kitchen/Bath, Appliances and More

NON-ALLOWABLE REPAIRS	Luxury Items	Structural, Additions, Major Repairs (Load Bearing Walls), Landscaping, Site Amenities, Uninhabitable Homes, Luxury Items	See Above	Landscaping, Site Amenities, Uninhabitable Homes, Luxury Items
APPRAISAL	HUD Consultants Specification of Repairs (SOR) Required to Order Appraisal	Contractors Bid Required to Order Appraisal. Must Breakdown Labor & Materials	Contractors Bid for Less than $50K Total. If over $50K Either a Consultant's Report or use of Granite Loan Management (GLM)	Contractors Bid Required to Order Appraisal. Must Breakdown Labor & Materials. Ordered thru V.A. Portal
SELF-HELP	Must Show Expertise. Cost of Labor Must be Included.	Must Show Expertise. May Require Consultant. Cost of Labor Must be Included.	Must Show Expertise. May Require Consultant. Cost of Labor Must be Included.	Not Allowed
CONTINGENCY RESERVE	10-20% Determined by Consultant	10% Utilities On 15% Utilities Off	10% or Determined by Consultant	Construction consultant required
CONSULTANT	HUD Consultant Required	None Required	Consultant Required If Structural Repairs or Repairs > $50,000	None Required
FINANCED MORTGAGE PAYMENTS	If Uninhabitable Consultant Must Notate Max 6 PITI Payments	None Allowed	If Uninhabitable Consultant Must Notate Max 6 PITI Payments	None Allowed
LEAD-BASED PAINT/TERMITE	Include in Repairs if Noted on Appraisal or Required by UW. *Must be EPA Certified to Remediate LBP		Termite Only: Include in Repairs if Noted on Appraisal or Required by UW	Include in Repairs if Noted on Appraisal or Required by UW. *Must be EPA Certified to Remediate LBP

CONTRACTOR	Must Fill Out Contractors Package and Provide at Least Two References, Liability Insurance, and Licensing Homeowner Contractor Agreement (HOCA) Must Be Executed Prior to Doc Signing			
# OF DRAWS	Up to 5 — No Initial Draw. 10% Hold back	Max 2 (Initial & Final)	No Consultant: 2 With Consultant: Max 5	Max 2 (Initial & Final)
TIME TO COMPLETE	6 Months	6 Months	6 Months	3 Months
DRAWN REQUEST TURN TIMES	INITIAL CHECK: 7-10 Calendar Days from COE I Interim Draws: 3 Days from Draw Inspection Received Final Check: 5-7 Days from notification of Completion			
ENERGY EFFICIENCY FUNDS (EEM)	Allows Borrowers to Finance Energy Efficient Upgrades to a Home in Addition to the Total Renovation Amount. This Includes Double-Paned Windows, Tank-less Water Heaters, Energy Efficient HVAC Systems, New Insulation, and More. Improvements Must be Cost Effective to be Included.			
	1-4 Unit Properties. Max 5% of the Property Value not to Exceed $8K. HERS Report Required.		1-4 Unit Properties. Max 10% of the "As Completed" Value. HERS Report Must Be Supplied to Appraiser.	1-4 Unit Properties. Up to $6K. HERS Report Required.
	Refer to Green Energy Guidelines for More Details			
MISCELLANEOUS	Supplemental Original Fee (Greater of $350 or 1.5% of total Renovation Costs)			Purchase Contract Must be Amended to Include Total Repair Costs and General List of Repairs

The Veteran Affairs Renovation

Veterans Affairs loans are for servicemen and women and their surviving spouses. With a VA renovation loan, you cannot abate the mortgage payment, and you must live in the house. This is not an investor loan. There is *no cap* on the number of repairs that can be done. Again, you will see a lot of lenders limit the number of repairs from lender to lender, so be careful when you are Internet surfing on that topic for this loan.

As with FHA loans, luxury items are not allowed. Most of the guidelines follow the FHA Consultant policies.

Karen C.

We have another example of a single mother buying her first home. She is a veteran and a firefighter—badass! She purchased a home on the same street she grew up on, and where her parents, aunt, uncle, and cousins still live. She had her eye on this home for years, but it needed *a lot* of work! She wanted to use her VA entitlement, but the house needed renovations. The lender she had been working with said the only way she could purchase this home was with an FHA 203(k). She didn't have the down payment saved, so 3.5 percent wasn't going to be easy to come by.

She was introduced to us, and we proceeded with a VA Renovation Loan with about $100,000 in rehab costs. The listing agent and other lenders warned everyone that VA renovation loans didn't exist, and then that they may exist, but never close. We certainly dispelled that myth. Her project is now complete, and she is living with her girls in a beautiful home on the same street she grew up on.

The Homestyle Renovation Loan

This loan is a conventional product that can do just about anything you can afford to do. The total project must validate the loan amount in the appraisal, but with as little as 5 percent down on primary residences, 10 percent down on second homes, and 15 percent down for investors.

With a Homestyle loan, you can do most things. You can raze a home and rebuild on an existing foundation, build outbuildings, put in a pool, add additional rooms, move a home, gut and reframe a structure, convert a building from a single to multi-family use, or finish an incompletely constructed home. As well, luxury items are allowed with Homestyle loans.

Hopefully, this chapter has helped you understand renovation loans more fully and decide which loan suits your needs the best. In the coming chapters, we will go into more detail about the renovation process.

CHAPTER 5: THE RENOVATION PROCESS (PART A)

"Good fortune is what happens when opportunity meets with planning."
Thomas Edison

If you have begun a renovation process on your own and have met with disaster, do not feel bad. It is not uncommon to encounter pitfalls in the renovation process, and we have sorted out several setbacks over the years. That is why we have developed a method for renovation lending that avoids common problems and helps to make the process go smoothly.

Disasters do happen, and they are most likely to occur when homeowners do not follow a set plan in the process of renovating their new homes under a renovation loan. We've seen several things go wrong for people who did not do a renovation loan process, and later on, called us for help.

Harrison bought a Hurricane Matthew house, which he'd been trying to fix up piecemeal with insurance money. He was trying to pay individual contractors and living in a construction zone. He finally was just about to give up, but he found a contractor to get him a bid and he called us for help. We were able to help him pay for the additional repairs and fix the house with a VA renovation loan as a refinance. We were also able to help him pull some cash out of the loan to pay his prior contractor. Once he had a loan and a plan, he was able to complete his renovations in a much more orderly manner. So, in this instance, the disaster was a natural one, but sometimes they are self-inflicted.

Courtney

"As a newbie realtor, shopping for my very first home with my husband, I knew it wasn't going to be easy finding the 'perfect' home in this very difficult and competitive market. Sure enough, we quickly realized that to win a bidding war on a turnkey house, we'd need to shop about $30,000-$50,000 below the top end of our budget to leave room for bidding. I felt that we were not getting a good bang for our buck. So, as a reno lover at heart, I started researching renovation loans and was utterly shocked at how many options were out there that I had never heard of before! I decided to pivot and began searching for homes that were fairly priced and needed some updating."

"Another realization I quickly had was that finding the right lender who was experienced in those types of loans was an absolute necessity. Thank God for the kind listing agent on the

home I fell in love with, who pointed me in the direction of Ron Byrom when another lender who had preapproved us for a reno loan failed us. Our renovation specialist picked up the pieces and from the moment I found him, the process to closing was seamless! I knew what was next every step of the way, and although I went into this process slightly intimidated, I felt confident and secure after beginning the journey with our renovation specialist and his team."

"Upon closing, based on the scope of work for the renovation, we had tens of thousands of equities already! Looking back, my husband and I know we did the right thing for us, and we love our home. We were able to work with an amazing general contractor and his team, Wright Homes, LLC; they took every Pinterest photo and crazy idea of mine and made it into a reality. We reconfigured the floor plan to add a half bath downstairs for guests, opened up the kitchen to living space, and now my kitchen is one of my favorites ever. We updated every single space in our home to reflect our style."

"We feel truly so blessed to have a home that we're proud of, and that we were able to customize to fit our specific needs. We shopped 'smarter' in this super-intense market and got the most potential for our budget. We couldn't be happier and wouldn't change a thing."

I have numerous stories like this one. One customer had a contractor tear off his roof before calling us, and the house sat in the rain and was virtually ruined. They were in the State of Florida, so they were able to be made whole by the state general fund and go after the contractor's license, but not without a little headache. Think about what that would have been like without the protection of a renovation loan.

We've had clients try to do unauthorized self-help where they could have included repairs. This buyer contracted someone to do all the major repairs required for a general appraisal condition. While in construction, he took it upon himself to take those repairs further by removing the kitchen, which they wanted to replace anyway. This was unauthorized work that the borrower wanted to do at his house. Unfortunately, he accidentally set the house on fire! Thank goodness we did have insurance in the process to make him whole inside the renovation loan.

We had a buyer who wanted to get around to doing a renovation loan and get a regular mortgage, and he gutted parts of the house before an appraiser came to see it. This had a sour effect that almost cost the buyer his purchase causing him to have to fix everything before closing. Think about your or the seller's exposure here and ask yourself if you'd put money into a home that you potentially may never close on. There are numerous ways not to do a renovation, and we've seen them all.

In this chapter, we will look at the preferred plan for doing a renovation loan. We have had experience with many loans, and this is the smoothest way forward to purchase and renovate a home using these loans.

Our Renovation Lending Method

Getting a renovation loan can seem complicated when you do not have experience in this area. Luckily, we have done many of these loans, and we have managed to work out an ideal way through the process, which we would like to share with you. Here, we will lay out our step-by-step method for buying a home using renovation loans. In the next section, we'll go through the steps in a little more detail.

The first thing you must do before all else, as with any home-buying process, is to get prequalified. You must partner with a competent lender to first determine your eligibility for financing. Do not get set on a house, budget, or even fixing any home until you know your budgetary limits and what type of financing you will need. This includes understanding the total out-of-pocket expense for closing *and* inspections before putting in a contract or even looking at a home.

The total monthly cost and the rate are just two components of financing when getting qualified. However, understanding your total cash for closing is possibly much more important to how your real estate professionals will assist you in obtaining a contract that works for you! After you are "pre-approved" with a lender, you may then proceed to these steps:

1) Get qualified for your loan. Figure out which loan suits your situation best: an FHA, VA, or Homestyle Renovation loan. Then, begin the application process for underwriting commitment.

2) Find the house you want. Follow my tips on how to do this in the next chapters.

3) Get an agent to help you write an offer commensurate with the market and home and get the home under contract.

4) Get a home inspection and HUD consultant. It's very important to do this before contractor estimates.

5) Get a contractor estimate for repairs you want to be done.

6) Have your HUD consultant and lender reviewed the estimate?

7) Order the appraisal for the future value of the home based on repairs.

8) Review the appraisal for any needed changes.

9) Go in for a final underwriting of the loan.

10) Close the loan.

11) Begin the repairs.

12) Consultant/appraiser confirms repairs.

13) Title to confirm no new liens on the property.

14) Contractor paid through the drawing process.

Know Which Loan Suits Your Situation Best

In Chapter 4, we went over the different types of loans that you can use for your renovation. You should begin the application process for a loan as early as possible. Identifying issues on your credit, monthly debts, and student loans should be dealt with before finding the dream home, as you want to be able to act quickly to put the house under contract when you do find the "right one."

If you don't have cash and are not approved, you may miss out on a chance of getting the home if you haven't been pre-approved. If you haven't spoken to a lender, and you feel confident that you can get on the phone easily you should shop around. I would also make certain you are working with someone that has had a lot of experience on the renovation loan if you think this is a possibility. This way, your lender can quickly pivot if they have to help you to get the home you want no matter what comes up in the process!

Find The House You Want

Finding a home can be a very difficult process. You may want to enlist the help of a good real estate agent to find a suitable candidate home in the area you want. When you are open to a renovation, it makes the process easier in several ways. The home does not have to be perfect as it is, and you can make a good equity position when you buy a home that needs some repairs. Your loan officer can pair you with a real estate professional who is good at finding these deals, and who also understands the renovation loan process.

Write An Offer Commensurate With The Market And Home

A licensed real estate agent can advise you on how to write the right offer for the home's present value. They are the professional who can help you with market analysis. They will understand the saturation rate of the market in the area, and they will know if the home is correctly listed for the area or if it is under-or overvalued.

An agent's knowledge is key to writing an offer that will be accepted by the seller so that you can get the home under contract. People often overlook the value of a great real estate agent in a transaction. This is why you should have someone represent you who you think will give you the best chances of getting under contract with the right home based on your fit with them.

Get A Home Inspection

I recommend using a HUD consultant who is also licensed to do home inspections. At a minimum, you need basic home inspections by a licensed home inspector. Although a HUD consultant is not required on all renovation loans, it can be useful to have them around for help with things like selecting a contractor or giving third-party advice on renovations. If you have any structural repairs or additions that are included in the scope of repairs, you are required to have a HUD consultant.

As well, if you want to abate the payment, or in other words, if you want to finance the mortgage payments because of the condition of the home and you don't want to live there during repairs, then you must have a HUD consultant. It's also handy in case you accidentally go over the amount you originally intended and would then need the consultant as an inspector. In this scenario, the consultant is already familiar with the project, which eliminates any delay.

This is the appropriate professional to give you a list of everything that needs to be done in the home and can also give you an idea of how much that is going to cost you. The HUD consultant can provide a SOR, or Specification of Repairs, which you will be able to use to get multiple bids from multiple contractors.

Get A Contractor Estimate For Repairs

I always recommend that you use a licensed, insured general contractor. The contractor needs to come to the house only after the home inspection because they do not want to have to make several visits to get an idea of what needs to be done so they can make a bid. The contractor must get subcontractors into the home so that they can come up with estimates for the final bid.

Using your HUD's specification of repairs, you can get estimates from many contractors if you so desire at this point. Instead of getting apples-to-oranges on quotes, the consultant's outline for repairs can be followed to ensure you secure apples-to-apples comparisons.

Have Your HUD Consultant And Lender Review The Estimate

You should get your HUD consultant to look over the bid first. They can make sure that all of the repairs that they specified are in there. If there's any ambiguity to the bid, they can fix it before having your lender review the bid. This can avoid needless delays and ambiguity with the appraisal, as we need to make the renovations clear so that the appraiser can give future value for the improvements.

Order The Appraisal For The Future Value Of The Home Based On Repairs

When you order the appraisal, you want to make sure that the appliances, electricity, gas, water, and utilities are on at the time of inspection. However, if you cannot have these things operational at this time, that is okay. Any suspected repairs will need to be articulated in the bid, and your consultant will have to inspect them when operational after closing to make sure they pass.

Furthermore, the appraisers will have to come back and review that everything is functioning at the final inspection. We even have an additional contingency in the renovation amount to make sure we have enough funds to complete the process.

Review The Appraisal

The appraiser and/or underwriter may cite some needed changes in the bid. They may spot something that has been missed, or they may have questions about something they see in the appraisal. You should review the appraisal, so you know about any needed changes with your loan officer.

Final Underwriting Of The Loan/Close The Loan

Next are steps 9 and 10. When the loan closes, the seller of the property gets paid. If it is a refinance, then your prior lender will be paid off and the renovation funds will be held back.

Your contractor does not get paid a lump sum of money at closing, which is generally what contractors prefer. In general, they will receive a small check at this time, unless they are doing a very small repair.

Begin The Repairs

At this time, renovations can begin on the home. This is the fun part where the magic begins to happen, and your fixer-upper starts to transform into your dream home.

Consultant/Appraiser Confirm Repairs /Title To Confirm No New Liens/Contractor Paid Through Draw Process

In steps 12, 13, and 14, the contractor gets paid as they complete repairs. The consultant will meet with the contractor to draw up a schedule together, so they will be on the same page as to what needs to be done and when. Every time the contractor needs to get paid, the financer will check with the title to make sure there are no new liens on the property before making payments.

For each draw, the consultant will arrive to review the house. At the very end, the appraiser will visit to make sure all the repairs are done. There will be one last title search on the property to check for liens before paying the contractor their final draw, and a waiver and release will be obtained.

Following The Plan: A Path To Success

You are now armed with a plan that will help you utilize renovation lending to achieve success. Find a trusted team, including real estate agents, lenders, home inspectors, contractors, real estate attorneys, and a certified public accountant. Choose a renovation loan that's right for you, and keep in mind the steps to follow that we outlined in this chapter.

This is your plan for leveraging renovation lending smoothly to achieve your dream home. In the next chapter, we will go into some more details about the process, including how to select the contractor that's right for you.

CHAPTER 6: THE RENOVATION PROCESS (PART B)

"The strength of the team is each individual member. The strength of each member is the team."
~ Phil Jackson

In the last chapter, we outlined the renovation process from selecting a home to paying your contractor through to the drawing approach. There are a few details that we want to expand on, and a few other details that we want to add. So, in this chapter, we are going to examine some things more thoroughly.

We will talk about selecting an experienced lender to help you through the renovation loan process. We will also discuss finding the right contractor, which can sometimes be one of the most difficult aspects of doing a renovation loan.

Once you have done these things, it is important for you and your contractor to know a few more details about the renovation process, such as getting paid through the draw system, the role of the HUD consultant, and where to find the total cost breakdown for your project.

Selecting A Lender

Many lenders do not want to deal with renovation loans because of their perceived level of difficulty. It can be a challenge to find a lender who is not only interested in taking on such a loan but also knows what they are doing.

By all means, you should try to find a lender that has experience with these types of loans. If you found out that you needed heart surgery, would you want an intern or a new doctor to take a crack at it? When you need a specialist, you should always understand their credentials before you engage them.

Ask your lender how many of these loans they have completed successfully. You may get only one chance to close a renovation loan in a competitive market. If you don't have the right lender to help you close on the first attempt, then you may not get a second try on a loan such as this. That is why it is vital to find a lender who has a track record and the systems in place to help customers through these processes.

Selecting A Contractor

Selecting a contractor may be one of the hardest parts of the renovation loan process. Many contractors may not be familiar with the process and will have to be brought "up to speed" with the details of working under a renovation loan. Not all contractors are a good fit for the renovation loan system, even if they are otherwise a great contractor.

To work with these loans, a contractor must meet certain criteria. Let's have a look at the contractor selection process and the drawing process for paying your contractor.

A contractor who is working on a renovation loan project must meet the following criteria:

1. They must be validated with state websites, with an active business and contractor licence as required at the state and/or municipal level.
2. They must possess General Liability insurance of $1,000,000 or greater. (Depending on the scope of the project, sometimes exceptions can be made to have a lower amount of liability insurance.) They must show proof of their insurance.
3. They need to have the means to complete the work and maintain their cash flow while awaiting payment draws, so they will need to carry an adequate reserve or line of credit for the project.
4. They may need to provide references, depending on the lender's preference.

5. They may need to include background or reference checks, again depending on the lender's preferences.

Some great contractors will not be a good fit for renovation loans because of their inability to fund a project or meet any of the above criteria.

A good contractor will already have some experience with this loan type. It is also a good idea to work with a contractor who can handle the administrative tasks of working with a HUD consultant and supply permits and other items to facilitate draws quickly, so you do not experience delays in the renovation process.

The contractor needs to understand the nuances of how renovation loans work before getting involved with the work. Doing so reduces the chance that your contractor will withdraw later in the project due to surprises.

Nuances Of Renovation Loans Your Contractor Needs To Know

There are a few details about renovation loans that your contractor needs to know before getting involved in the project. First, and probably most important, payment is not done upfront. A contractor is paid in a draw process, after submitting a bid and completing portions of the work on the bid that will be inspected. The draw process is outlined below.

Due to the complexity of this arrangement, and the nature of renovation loans in general, there will likely be more paperwork that the contractor will have to complete and sign than they are typically used to on a project. Also, timeframes for getting work done will have to be laid out explicitly beforehand.

The contractor of record must sign the bid for the work to be completed. Someone cannot "use the contractor's licence." The contractor does have the ability to subcontract the work to whoever they like based on the bid outlined in the scope of work.

Verbal agreements with the contractor should be set down in writing in the bid to avoid any issues. You do not want to have an argument later over builder-grade cabinets versus custom cabinets, and when you refer back to the bid it does not specify, and you end up with a lower grade product. If it is important enough to talk about, then it should be written down.

The Draw Process

Draws are set forth by the lender based on the type of renovations, type of loan, loan amount, and scope of repairs. To determine the initial disbursement amount, depending on the type of loan, the lender will likely want the contractor's bid to be broken out by the scope of work per project and by the labour and materials involved.

The draw process will take a few days to perform. Typically, a draw is accompanied by an inspection by a HUD consultant or appraiser. The lender will also get an updated title search to ensure there are no other claims on the title before paying the contractor.

For a limited project, the contractor will receive an initial disbursement after the loan funds. Final payment will be issued as long as the lender has all the closing documents and a passing final inspection. The borrower or contractor should contact their lender when the project is complete with a final invoice, showing how much, they have been paid, how much they are owed, and any change of work from the original scope.

Note that any change of work should not take place until the lender has approved it. Otherwise, the funds may have to come out of pocket for the customer.

In a standard project, the consultant is the person who will drive the draw process. Once the contractor completes 20 percent of the scope, they can request that the consultant do a draw inspection. They will need to provide an invoice showing what work has been completed and needs to be inspected. Once a successful inspection has been done, the consultant will put together the necessary paperwork that can be submitted to the lender to draw the funds, which will be signed by the consultant, borrower, and contractor.

The write-up from the consultant helps break things down for draws. If there is no write-up from a consultant, the bid needs to be clear enough to facilitate draws accurately as work is completed. We'll talk a little more about the contractor's bid below.

The Consultant

Who is the consultant? Usually, a consultant is an appraiser or a HUD consultant. A HUD consultant is designated by the Department of Housing and Urban Development to help with renovation loan draws and to identify mandatory repair items and minimal HUD standards. They can help in putting together your scope of work. A HUD consultant can be licensed to do home inspections. They act as a disinterested third party so they can be an advocate for you, the customer. As we discussed in previous chapters, a HUD consultant can help in selecting a contractor.

The Contractor's Bid

The contractor's bid is a document in which the contractor lays out a narrative that explains exactly what work is to be done and how. A good bid should explain what trims and finishes are considered and should list each project separately. Within each project, the bid should contain a breakout of labour and materials.

This is not to see how much profit the contractor is making. Rather, it is useful to see what the percentage of materials is, as those numbers can aid in getting the contractor funds for the project because this can determine the amount of money that can be advanced before completion. A material draw is sometimes allowed for certain loans, and if the lender does not know the cost of materials, they cannot determine this draw.

Below, we have included some examples of contractor bids. You will note that there is a "better bid", which is detailed in narrating the work to be done, the quantity, and cost of repairs (although it does not lay out the cost of materials vs. labour), and a "bad bid", which does not provide much detail at all, but only addresses total costs. The contractor needs to make sure that the bid is as detailed as possible. The first bid could be improved by including a breakdown of materials and labour, and the second bid needs a great deal more information.

Example of a Bad Bid

Item	Description	Unit Price	Sub Total	Total
1	Painting		$500.00	
2	Fencing		$750.00	
3	Exterior Doors		$1000.00	
4	Trim		$250.00	
5	Flooring		$5000.00	
6	Plumbing		$450.00	
7	Electrical		$825.00	
8	Cabinetry		$3000.00	
9	Appliances		$5000.00	
10	Misc.		$1500.00	
11	Bath Repair and Renovation (Drywall, Carpentry, Tile, Plumbing, Fixtures, Accessories		$5400.00	
				$23,675.00

Example of a Good Bid

General Conditions	Qty	Cost
REMOVE ROT & TERMITE DAMAGED EXTERIOR WOOD SIDING REPLACING W/ 5/16" X 8.25 HARDIE SIDING 3 PIECES RIGHT OF THE GARAGE ENTRY. 12 PIECES RIGHT OF THE BAY KITCHEN WINDOW. REPLACE 2X6 AND 2X4 CEDAR TRIM ON KITCHEN, DINING, AND MASTER SILLS, 5' SECTION ON FRONT RIGHT OF HOUSE AT 8' FLASHING, AND 3 VERTICAL TRIP PIECES AT FRON CORNER OF HOUSE AT BAY WINDOW AND CORNER OF GARAGE	75LF	$282.00
REPAIR AND EXTEND DOWNSPOUTS (2) 2X3 TRANSITION ELBOSE, (2) 2X3 DOWNSPOUT EXTENSIONS, AND ADD (2) 24" STONE COLOR SPLASHGUARDS ON FRONT AND BACK RIGHT OF HOUSE	2 ITEMS	$322.00
PAINT BODY AND TRIM W/ LEXON AND SEALKRETE	1,230SF	$1,150.00
REMOVE EXISTING ROOF SHINGLES, REPLACE WITH ARCHITECTURAL SHINGLES TO MATCH EXISTING DUPLEX NEIGHBOR. 30 LB FELT, 5 NEW LEAD BOOTS, 3 GOOSENECKS, 200 LF OF TAN DRIP EDGE, 2 RIDGE VENTS	2,479SF	$4,779.00
DISPOSAL 20 YARD DUMPSTER	20 YARDS	$275.00
ENTRY DOOR- KS JUNO COMBO AND DEADBOLT, SATIN NICKEL	1 ITEM	$128.00
GARAGE ENTRY -KS JUNO COMBO KNOB AND DEADBOLT SET	1 ITEM	$50.00
GARAGE DOOR – 10 NYLON ROLLERS, 19 #2 HINGE	I ITEM	$302.00
HVAC		
COMPLETE SYSTEM P.M TO INCLUDE HONEYWELL DIGITAL PROGRAMMABLE THERMOSTAT.	BASIC	$300.00
CLEAN INDOOR COIL PURGE CONDENSATE LINE	BASIC	INCLUDED ABOVE

Total Renovation Costs And The Maximum Mortgage Worksheet

At the end of the day, what is included in the total renovation cost? The contractor's bid provides a good starting point, but it doesn't cover everything. The best place to see an illustration of the total project is the Maximum Mortgage Worksheet. Here, you will see the bid, soft costs to pay for inspections, the costs to service the draws, payment abatement, and contingency reserve.

The Maximum Mortgage Worksheet allows you to understand the total project financed amount, down payments, and a breakdown of all the funds used for the project. The Contingency Reserve is there in case you have any cost overruns for the project or run into any projects that may require additional funding. If any of the soft costs or contingencies are not used, the fund goes back down to the principal balance of the loan.

Final Items To Note

Allow yourself time for closing on these loans. Traditionally, the closing dates on a normal loan are about 30 days. These timeframes should be extended on a renovation loan based on the contractor's estimate. Allow 45 days for these loans to close.

You will want to make sure that you have all the home's appliances and utilities operational when the home is inspected. If the utilities cannot be turned on, you should assume anything might be wrong with a condition on the property to ensure your bid contains all the necessary projects to complete your home. In some instances, a generator is used to test the electricity, and the pipes are pressure tested with a compressor on a water pipe where the water cannot be turned on.

We do not recommend self-help on these projects unless it is for minor items like plugging in your appliances or a painting job. If you are in a licensed trade, like a plumber or general contractor, then that is a different matter, but for most people, it is just not a good idea. We always recommend the work be done under a properly insured, licensed general contractor.

Enjoying The Renovation Process

The renovation can be the most fun part of the entire renovation loan process. After all, who doesn't enjoy customizing a home to their tastes and standards, and watching that customization take shape as the contractors do their work? It is extremely rewarding to step into your new home and enjoy all the details that you planned and laid out perfectly and professionally.

In these chapters, we have tried to help make the process as smooth and comfortable as possible by laying out the details for you based on our extensive experience. Take your time, make notes, and be sure to plan your renovation loan process beforehand, and enjoy the renovation experience.

CHAPTER 7: HOW TO MARKET DISTRESSED PROPERTIES

"Some people look for a beautiful place, others make a place beautiful."
~ Hazrat Inayat Khan

Susan could not figure out why her house would not sell. It was in a good area of the city, close to shops and parks, and it had everything a buyer could want: three bedrooms, a garage, a backyard, and even a room that could be used for an office. Sure, it had never been renovated since it was built in the 1970s, but a buyer could easily do that, couldn't they?

She sighed as she locked the front door after her fourth open house. The house had been on the market for two years. When prospective buyers had come in, they had looked at the orange shag carpet and the crowded little kitchen and shook their heads. They stood outside, examined the roof, and they balked. Susan thought that maybe she could do some small renovations, like painting, but she knew she couldn't afford to change the floor plan into an open plan, improve the kitchen, install wood floors, and redo the roof. What was she going to do?

She thought about it on her drive home. Today she decided to take a different route, to see another house that she'd found in the local listings. The house had just gone up for sale not too far away from her own house, and she wanted to check it out since it was competition.

Right away, when she arrived at the house for sale, she noticed something. The sign out front said, "Call John Adams* to discuss special renovation loans for this property to include all repairs and improvements."

There was a lady at the front door, just entering the house, so Susan pulled up and waved. The lady smiled at her. "I'm Rachel," she said. "I'm the real estate agent for this listing. I was just going in to check on something, would you like to look around?"

Why not, Susan thought. She accepted the offer and had a look inside. To her surprise, the house was in worse shape than hers. It was in obvious need of renovation, with dirty old carpets and smoke-stained paneling on the walls. Not only did it need a new roof, but it could do with an entire gut on the first floor. She thanked the realtor and drove home thoughtfully.

Susan kept an eye on the listing and was shocked when, two weeks later, the house sold. She made up her mind and called the number on the sign. She chatted with the friendly team member who answered and set up a meeting. Before long, she had learned a great deal about renovation lending, and she got a sign of her own to put in front of her house.

She found a contractor to price out the needed renovations to her home and included his estimate with the literature on renovation loans that she left in the kitchen for prospective buyers to peruse and take home. Then, she changed the wording in her listings to make them more renovation–friendly by inviting the reader to "Customize this home with renovation financing".

Susan had several new, interested home buyers—and a few familiar faces—come to visit the home over the next few weeks. She was truly gratified to sell the house two weeks later and was able to progress to the next stage of her life by moving to a new home out of state.

Why Distressed Homes Do Not Sell

Frequently, distressed homes sit on the market for an excessive amount of time and do not sell. Why is this? In a competitive market, such homes require a different approach.

A lot of listings of distressed homes are not aimed at a wide enough audience. In our case above, Susan listed her home as a "Fixer Upper" needing some "TLC".

Prospective buyers came in and saw outdated décor and an old roof and imagined many problems behind the walls. Buyers had the option of choosing other homes that did not need so much work, and so they did.

"Fixer Upper", "Needs TLC", "Calling all investors", and "Cash Only" are just some examples of listings that tend to dramatically reduce the number of people that will be interested in a house because they imagine that the home comes with all sorts of problems that they don't know how to fix, and they are unwilling to take the risk.

How To Increase Potential Buyers For Your Home

When you say in your listing that a home is for investors, then you will drive away potential occupants. Equally, you may drive away occupants with terms like "Fixer Upper" because many people view fixing up a house to be an insurmountable challenge.

You should try to expand your market for your distressed home so that it is as wide as possible. Keep in mind that you want to attract occupant home buyers, not just investors. Occupant home buyers are great for neighborhoods and home values. Home occupants will fix a house up more than an investor will and will generally care for the home a little better. Furthermore, they will probably be interested in paying more for the home than an investor would.

You need to show the occupant home buyer that there is a way in which they can become a happy homeowner of your distressed home. Too often, they may look at the problems posed by a distressed home and turn away. It is thus your job to provide them with a bridge to show them that home ownership is possible by talking to them about renovation lending.

There are several strategies for marketing your distressed home so that it will be noticed by buyers who might be interested in renovation lending.

Educate Your Buyers

This can be done in several ways. The sign that Susan saw in front of the house to be sold in her neighborhood is one way to direct buyers to call a renovation lender, who can educate them on the various renovation loan products that make a distressed home accessible. She also doesn't have to explain the process to everyone, as her lender will do this for her.

You can add a sign, or verbiage in your listing, which says things like "Customize this home with renovation finance" or "Include all customization and personalization of this home in your purchase". Include a phone number to direct people to call your renovation lender, who can educate them about renovation financing.

It is important to remember to include a method for your customers to contact the renovation lender. Your real estate agent may not be well versed in renovation lending and may not want to go into detail about it with a prospective buyer. If your agent can hand the buyer the relevant literature and direct them to the source (the lender), this will create a smoother experience for everyone involved. The lender can then explain renovation financing to the potential customer, and when they are done, the lender can redirect the customer to the listing agent who can show them the house.

Literature and flyers about renovation lending can be left on the kitchen counter of a home for sale for buyers to peruse at their leisure and included in the package of documents that you give a prospective buyer. It is a great idea to include in your documents both lending literature and a contractor's bid for the work to be done because this gives people a real feel for what is possible.

Show And Tell

If you bring a contractor into the house to give you an idea of what can be done with it, and provide an estimate, this can be a great tool to draw in prospective buyers. A printout of the prospective plan for the renovations on the counter gives potential buyers something to imagine. It can also go in the document set that is given to agents and buyers, along with the material about renovation financing.

You could get samples of granite for the new kitchen counter and paint chips and lay those out. This way, people can touch the materials and visualize what could happen in their minds. It is useful to evoke peoples' imaginations and their senses when trying to pitch them the sale of a distressed home. Most people cannot imagine well for themselves what a home would look like with renovations, but if you add diagrams and samples, you can boost their conceptions significantly, and thus improve the appeal of the home.

If I tell you the roof needs replacing, that isn't very sexy. However, if you can see the shingles of the new roof and the plan, and you can see a document that says that fixing the roof will lower your insurance premium, then suddenly it is exciting. Outline to prospective buyers all the possible changes and show them explicitly with diagrams and materials what can be done. This will boost their interest exponentially.

For Realtors

When prospective home buyers have a question about renovation lending, they may ask the first person at hand, who is often the real estate agent. If you are a real estate agent, and you are interested in getting to know more about renovation lending so that you can help your clients with a better level of service, then you have already begun the process by picking up this book. That is a great start.

We also offer a three-hour continuing education (CE) class to realtors in the State of Florida, which we have taught to over 8,000 agents in the last twelve years. You can earn three hours of CE and gain an in-depth understanding of renovation lending.

We also offer a 45-minute seminar on the renovation process and everything you need to know to get through it on our website at JohnAdamsteam.com.

CHAPTER 8: BEYOND THE SINGLE HOUSE HACK

"The best investment on Earth is earth."
~ Louis Glickman

Do you dream of becoming independent through real estate ownership? Do you imagine yourself vacationing in your second home in the mountains or on the beach someday in the future? Do you envision owning a string of rental properties? Renovation lending can make these dreams a reality.

I remember my wife leaving the first house I bought one July night to stay at her parents' house. I had not been able to get the air conditioner working for a couple of days. If anyone has lived in Florida in July without an AC, you kind of know why. This was before learning to house hack, and the house was in the middle of a renovation. I was doing it all the wrong way on my own without a GC or direction. It is one of many examples where I lost money. Your first house shouldn't be the hardest, and I went about it all wrong.

The very first house I financed after learning house hacking was my most successful hack. I grew up just down the street from this house and played in the woods behind it. It was a home of fantasy because it was so big, old, and had a commanding presence looking over to the beach and sitting on a huge lot. The home had sat on the market overpriced and under-marketed for a few years after the crash. I was able to work out a deal with the seller to buy the home at a good value and put over $140,000 in repairs into it with an FHA loan.

I lived there for a decade with my wife and children and was able to play at the beach and enjoy the pool we built. Recently, we sold the home for almost triple what we had paid for it. One of the best hacks I can think of is legally not paying taxes on real estate gains. Because it was my homestead property and I lived there for the required amount of time per the IRS code, I was exempt for up to $500,000 for this sale. That's like making $800,000 and not paying taxes! These funds leveraged me into more real estate and more investments.

When I started buying homes, I looked for whatever made money more so than what moved me emotionally. I suggest looking for opportunity rather than "the perfect home". This gives you a leg up on searching for an opportunity that could use some sort of fix immediately or over time to your profit.

The next house hack involves buying for primary intent. In this case, you're going to live in the house for one to two years. However, your ultimate objective is to buy a home and keep it; then, rent it out and buy your next primary. My friend Brendan Donelson wrote a book called *Never Sell Your First Home* that discusses this same theme. I have had the privilege to help several young investors do this six times over, and they are now wealthy landlords. This includes a local produce manager at my favorite local grocery store, and he is only 29!

We will explore other investment avenues in this chapter, such as BRRR (buy, rehabilitate, rent, and refinance), and fix and flip. We will also touch on the 1031 exchange, which is an investment strategy to help you make your money go further as a real estate investor.

The Multifamily House Hack

A multifamily home can be quite a few things. It might be an apartment building, but equally, it might be a duplex or quadruple-plex home. It can even be a home with an accessory dwelling, like a mother-in-law suite, or an apartment over the garage that you can rent out. It is something that you can use to reduce or net-zero the cost of living in your own home.

If I lost everything tomorrow and had to do it all over again, my first home would be a multifamily unit. There is money out there to rehabilitate a multifamily house, and, by the definition of house hacking, it is a way to net-zero your cost of living through real estate investments.

So, if I was just buying my first home, I would try to find a multifamily house because it accomplishes the mission of producing rental income while you live there. How is it different? It sets you up for future success in all your real estate ventures because the minute you move out of it (or if you stay there), you are going to increase all that rent you were not paying. This is because the renter was allowing you to live at net-zero with another renter. Thus, you are only going to make more money on the house.

Chris was an active-duty military person and found a home in the downtown district that was a quadplex. He was able to buy the home and include all the needed repairs. Then, he lived in one unit and rented out the other three. Instantly, upon leasing out the other units, he was making a positive cash flow on a home he lived in still and was getting paid to live there. When he receives orders to move in a few years, he will rent out his unit and remain profitable while moving on to the next home using his remaining entitlement. In other words, he can use his VA benefit more than once, which is a fact that most people do not know.

Honestly, buying a single-family home is not an investment; it is a liability. You have to pay for it every month, and there is no guarantee you are going to make equity from it (although it's likely if you hold onto it for the long term). Most people are still caught up in the equity dream, but if the financial crisis of 2007 and 2008 taught us anything, it was that we cannot rely on such things. If you have a roommate, you can house hack, too, and defray a monthly payment, but just not on a larger scale. These are all ways to increase cash flow while you establish a home.

Daniel bought a house when he was 19 years old. His dad helped him out with the down payment, and he bought a home that needed a lot of work. He then had his brother and another roommate move into the other two bedrooms. Between the two other rental incomes, he made the house payment with the two rents and created a ton of equity by buying a home that needed a lot of work. He still resides there today, and we just closed on a vacation rental property for him. He used some of the equity to install a pool and placed the down payment on the investment property.

A multifamily home, however, is a different story. It brings you money through rent and predictable cash flow, so it is a real investment even if you are living in one of the units. Equity is not income. Income is income. If you can truly cash flow your property in any market, then rent is typically going to go up. It's never going to go down to zero.

The Second House Hack

I have bought several second homes. I keep buying and selling them. I'll buy them, and then I will go on vacation with my family there. I will spend some time fixing the home up, relaxing, and then renting it out when I'm not there. So, I cover the costs of owning the house by renting it out periodically. In some seasons, I make a ton of money, but it is cyclical. The acquisition and enjoyment of the property is my main motivation for buying these types of properties. With rising values, I have had to take profits on some of those properties, and always have a sharp eye out on an area I wouldn't mind living in during some of my off time.

The whole idea is to have a place that you can enjoy. You will probably make some equity, and you are going to defray the cost of ownership by being able to rent the property out on occasion. Many times, you can find distressed and deeply discounted deals on rural area homes or cabin-type communities.

Jeremey and his family wanted to travel out to the springs here in Florida. They found a great deal on a foreclosure that needed some easy fixes. The house was right across the street from a popular state park entrance and was located on eight acres. Not only did it have a house and land, but it also had hookups for five RV stations on the property. They were thus able to transform the house into a cool second home for family vacations. They were also able to generate income by renting the RV pads out for short-term rentals.

Examples Of The Multifamily And Second House Hacks

I have several examples of multifamily and second house hacks that have made people a lot of money. Here are a couple of my favorites.

Neil bought a 61-unit apartment complex with two other investor friends right out of college. His circumstance was very unique, but it does show you that he was able to buy his "first home" where he lived and managed the units. Neil was able to produce an income based on ownership, and he completely paid for and profited off this first home. This project also springboarded him into several other projects in which he was able to leverage income and equity.

This is extremely fortunate and an exception to the rule. Special financing considerations were made on a commercial-type loan, and these young adults were backstopped with a ton of cash. There are a lot of folks suggesting that novice real estate investors go big or go home, but from someone who has done it, I can tell you that there are more big risks than rewards. If you don't have a sound plan and cash to back you up, then I suggest a slow and methodical climb to the top of your real estate investing.

Fourteen years ago, I was just getting my chapter 7 bankruptcy from the mistakes I made in my former real estate investments. Not every deal I have done has been a success since then. Still, I have had enough wins and enough small losses that I can say real estate is what turned me into a wealthy American from a bankrupt 27-year-old at the time of the collapse. It takes time, but I am living proof that you can systematically build a portfolio on any budget and credit.

Stephanie bought a second home in North Carolina that had a detached garage with a bathroom and loft apartment. She included all the repairs in the deal. So, she was able to spend time in the mountains with her family and have extra room for other guests, besides making some equity on the home. When she wasn't using the home, she had a local rental company manage the property and was able to break even on the payments to net zero her ownership of the home.

The BRRR Method

BRRR stands for buy, rehabilitate, rent, and refinance. There's another R (repeat), but it seems excessive. I like this approach a bit less than our method of renovation lending, and I will explain why.

BRRR(R) was created in the book *Rich Dad Poor Dad* by Robert Kiyosaki. It is a method of investing in real estate that is meant to grow your money by buying, rehabilitating, renting out, and refinancing your property. Having leverage in real estate means being able to own your property and, over time, have an asset that you can borrow from tax-free. This is where Kiyosaki's term fits in.

Buying with this method involves purchasing low, so that means finding a property that needs a lot of cosmetic upkeep or repairs. For every hundred homes you look at, you might find one that's perfect for your needs. This will be easy *if* you have the cash for the loan to buy that house *and* the cash for the repairs.

If you don't have cash for repairs, then the rehabilitating part also involves financing the rehab. You put it in the down payment. If you rehab, under Kiyosaki's method, you are putting all the cash for the rehab either on your credit cards or taking money out of your pocket. I believe that using cash is lazy when you can borrow and leverage the money, so perhaps you might look for different methods of financing the rehab.

Now that you have bought the property and placed all this money into it, you need to put a renter in there. In the banking world, they like this scenario because they can see that you have rehabbed the property and you have cash flowing. Thus, they are happy to loan you the money. This means you can refinance. Now you can cash out, and you do not get taxed on loans, which is a great investment hedge. You then maintain the rental and grow your money over time, while taking the cash out and famously repeating the process.

There are a couple of problems with the BRRR method in my opinion. One is that you have put out all this cash, and you do not know how long it is going to take to get it back or even if you can!

With a renovation loan, though, we analyze all the costs upfront, and we do not assume what needs to be done. The lender protects you through the process, holding the money back to pay the licensed, insured contractor when the work is done.

A renovation loan will give you a future value, whereas with BRRR you are assuming this value.

With the refinance, in a BRRR there is an assumption that the house is going to be worth more, and that you are going to get the cash back from the sale. However, this is not necessarily true. What if you have a tax return issue or qualification problem later down the road because of title seasoning? With title seasoning, you must wait for about six months until you can get the money back out of the house. Who knows what will happen in the market between now and then?

What if you get laid off, have tax issues, miss a bill payment (leading to a lower credit score), or some other kind of life event? Now, you cannot get your cash back. I have had to counsel people who have done it this way, and it can be scary because such problems in life do happen. That is why this method is scary for me. It's also pretty expensive, as most of the exotic financing vehicles we just talked about usually have higher rates and costs. In addition, the cost of refinancing depletes profits and equity.

So, BRRR allows you to buy, renovate, rent, refinance, and then do it all over again. However, as an investor or someone who wants to live in the house, the renovation loan gives you more bang for your buck, and with less risk. BRRR is great, but renovation loans are better because they accomplish the same things in one loan and one step without all the risk.

Fix And Flip

The fix and flip approach is very popular today. It is where people buy homes that are dated, and they need to be fixed up to look pretty. In most cases, they do not change the bones of the house and are not adding long-term value to it. It is an equity gain, done most of the time with hard money, and it is usually time-sensitive because you are relying on the market not to change while you renovate the house. This means you have to work fast.

In addition, you have to pay capital gains every time you get into and out of a transaction. With so many taxes to pay, you have to make your profit in volume, and that means you have to flip several houses. Often, third-rate contractors are used, and the work is not done very well.

There is a lot of personal liability to doing a fix and flip. Should something go wrong, lawyers can and will come after you, even if you are working under a corporation. With a renovation loan, you are working with licensed contractors, which reduces or eliminates this risk.

There is also speculation as to what the future value of the house will be, which adds a lot of uncertainty and risk to the transaction. This is not an issue with a renovation loan, where you already know the future value of the house before you even begin the work.

The 1031 Exchange

The 1031 exchange is named after Section 1031 of the U.S. Internal Revenue Code. It allows you to basically swap the equity and profit from the sale of one investment property to purchase another of like kind and defer capital gains taxes.

Certain rules must be met in the transaction, so you need a good tax professional and real estate attorney to guide you. You would need a Qualified Intermediary to take the money from the sale of the first property at closing and hold it, dispersing it to the new escrow agent when you meet the timelines set forth for buying the next property. You mustn't sell or take the funds without first setting up 1031, or else you could be subject to taxation.

The 1031 exchange is a great way to keep your dominoes going if you are a real estate investor. Used in a trust format, it can basically defer taxes for a long time for you and your heirs. However, and this is a big caveat, they must be paid at some point by someone. If you are looking to sell or move investments, this strategy can help you use more of your profits for the next project rather than putting it toward taxes.

A personal example of using this method to keep profits going would be a second home purchase we did in North Carolina. We later decided to rent it out, and one of the tenants wanted to buy it. We would have made almost $100,000 on the profit and would have been subject to about 35 percent of those funds being taxed. Instead, we found two duplexes to buy. So, rather than making a marginal profit on rents (or just taking cash on the sale), we were able to buy two income-producing properties, and that cash flowed a lot better.

Later, one of those duplexes was sold and we again did a 1031 exchange to a condo that we rented out as a vacation rental. Again, we deferred the taxes and leveraged it to another property with more income. Here, we didn't pay the taxes right away, and because of that, we had more money to invest in the next home to leverage into a better investment. Had we paid the taxes right away, we wouldn't have been able to diversify into several other homes that were making money.

What Not To Do

There are some things that sound just too good to be true. The thing is, if you feel that way about it, then you are probably right. There are many people out there teaching many things, and some of them are questionable. Some of the sensational ideas that are being sold to thousands of new investors could get you prison time. Therefore, it is vitally important to select a team that will keep you out of trouble.

In the 1980s, people used to do a thing called a *wraparound mortgage*, where the seller holds the mortgage for the buyer and holds all the profit and equity of the sale. The buyer then makes the mortgage payment to the seller. The seller then makes the payment to the bank. This is not something I would encourage. This is supposed to trigger many "due on sale" clauses in your mortgage.

I would also exercise caution with tax lien sales. This is a great way to buy a home if you are informed, have someone who can check the title for you, and you have the cash. However, the person you are buying from can come to collect the home sometime in the next seven years under certain circumstances, so there are risks. You'll need an advanced real estate team if you are looking for these opportunities. These are usually better ideas for people who have a lot of cash on hand for these types of transactions.

One myth I have kept hearing since I thought about getting into real estate is that you can buy real estate with no money down. I believe this is just poor guidance. This is also reckless advertising for the unsuspecting consumer. If you do not have the money to put down for even a basic home inspection and appraisal, then you should probably rethink your decision to buy real estate at this time.

The truth is that if you get under contract on a home, then you could very well find out something is wrong with a home that would make you not want to purchase it. There is also a chance the home may not appraise. If this happens, no one is going to reimburse you. It may be money well spent though to find out then the house isn't for you. There are all kinds of pieces of advice like this out there, and I urge that you take them all with caution.

The takeaway lesson here is that real estate does take a little planning, money, and hard work. If anyone is telling you that they can bypass these things, then be careful. Maybe they have found a great method, but probably not. Trust your instincts. If you want to invest in real estate, then you should be prepared to do the work.

However, if you are willing to put in the hours and invest time and money, then real estate can work out. I know this because I have done it. I have seen renovation lending work out for a lot of people, and I have seen people make money in real estate. It is possible. Do your research, pull up your sleeves, and you can achieve success!

CHAPTER 9: BRINGING IT HOME

"Every accomplishment starts with the decision to try."
~ Gail Devers

We have come a long way in this book, building from the ground up a vision of what you can do with some research and planning to invest in the best ways possible in real estate. In the early chapters, we learned a lot about house hacking, renovation lending, and the modern housing market. In today's market, being open to renovations and renovation lending is a great way to get your foot in the door of real estate because there are so many homes and properties out there that just need some modernization and fixing up to meet your needs. With just as much emphasis, though, we also talked about things to watch out for.

There are various kinds of renovation loans available to help begin your journey into real estate that can be tailored to suit your particular needs. In Chapter 4, we outlined them all to give you an idea of what they look like. In Chapters 5 and 6, we discussed a process for using renovation loans to rehabilitate a property, so that you could gain an appreciation for the steps involved. Finally, in the following chapters, we looked at ways of marketing your distressed properties, and we also talked about real estate beyond the single house hack: what to do when you're interested in dealing with being a landlord, and/or owning multiple properties.

Where to go next? In this chapter, I would like to introduce a simple plan for the next steps that you need to take after you put this book down. If you have gotten this far, and you're excited to begin your real estate career, here is some straightforward advice.

1. Build Relationships

Relationships will be important to everything you do in real estate. Remember when we talked about building your team in Chapter 3? These relationships will also see you through the complicated ins and outs of lending and renovating, not only for a single-family home but if you are interested in building multiple types of estate ventures, like a portfolio of rental homes or apartments. There is nothing more valuable than the knowledge of people in the business who are experienced in doing this work.

You will need to build and nurture relationships throughout every part of your real estate experiences. From educating yourself about real estate to planning your business to building a team of professionals to help you with your real estate ventures, your relationships with others will be key to your success in all aspects of this business.

Leverage the relationships that you build. Find friendly experts and use their experience and knowledge as you expand your real estate business. Examine your relationships and try to find the people who are putting your best interests at heart. These are the people you want to build relationships with.

It is, unfortunately, true that sometimes the people you meet may not have your best interests at heart, and you will have to learn to figure out when this is the case. Some people are just great salesmen, and they can hook you like they would a fish on a line. Be careful not to fall for their banter. Ask yourself: Would this person be willing to go an extra mile for me? Are they willing to teach me the things I don't know, even when I don't know how to ask them to do this?

With relationships, as with every part of your plan, sometimes you just must go with your gut to make decisions. This is okay, but you should always have a plan and an exit strategy. If you must make a coin flip, which may happen, always err on the side of caution. Some of the best deals I've gotten into have been because of the relationships I have had. I've gotten word about a property about to come on the market, or someone thinking about selling, or an opportunity that wasn't public yet. Relationships can uncover great opportunities!

2. *Educate Yourself*

So many investors today simply educate themselves insufficiently. They take a single web-based seminar, hear something from a friend, take barstool real estate advice, or, worst of all, bet on appreciation for the wealth creation and decision-making of their purchase. Real education is a much more involved process, no matter how you go about it. Dig in, take notes, and ask questions. The best question you should ask professionals is "What am I not asking that I should?"

As a first step, I recommend you check to see if you have a local real estate investors group. Attend a meeting to get a feeling of whether home ownership is the right thing for you. If you plan to become a landlord someday, this is a great way to meet others who are venturing into their first few investments or are very experienced people. This may solidify that you just want to live in a home without being an investor, and that is okay—it's a learning experience! Being a landlord isn't for everyone, but these groups can help you identify good deals.

Talk to people in your circle of influence but take their words with a grain of salt. I have known college graduates who have come out of economics schools to fail in business, and unseasoned financial planners who have never owned a home try to advise people on real estate matters. Listen to people but try to understand where they are coming from. Are they an expert with years of experience under their belt? Or do they have a little experience and lots of ideas, some of which may be useful and some which may not?

Sometimes, having the most experience isn't the most important thing. At times, it can be more important that the person you are talking to is willing to understand your unique situation and tell you the things you did not know to ask about. These people are very valuable sources of information because they get to know you and they are truly interested in helping you.

Books are a great source of education. There are many books out there, several of which have great ideas. Again, though, it is crucial to take such opinions with a little caution. For example, you can look for reviews about the book. Do reviewers think the ideas are good? Who are the reviewers? Are they real estate experts? Are they people who benefitted from the advice given in the book? I highly recommend anything by Robert Kiyosaki (*Rich Dad Poor*

Dad, Warner Books, 2000). His approach to owning real estate is very similar to my own beliefs on assets and using debt to make you wealthy. Also, the previously mentioned *Never Sell Your First Home* by Brendan Donelson is a fantastic first-time read.

Educating yourself is about actively reaching out and finding the best sources of knowledge about real estate that you can. Whether these be seminars or classes, local group meetings, people you meet, or books, you should immerse yourself in your education. Learn as much as you can, within a reasonable time frame, so that you can feel more confident in your decisions later on.

Along the way, you are likely to meet someone who has done the things you are looking to do in real estate. Find someone who has a similar vision and goals and look to them as a mentor. I didn't have a mentor when I got into real estate, but now I do. These folks will help you out and occasionally pass on a deal that they may not have the capacity for. You may thus have a windfall based on your association with them.

3. *Plan*

In its most meager beginnings, Walmart thought itself out and planned for growth very well, and now it is a multibillion-dollar business. It was so well planned out that its founder thought ahead to hold the company as a trust, which conferred certain advantages. When we enter real estate, we too should plan ahead. We should have a system for financing/cash, how we hold the title, and what exit strategy we have for our investment. When we begin purchasing real estate, we should begin with the end in mind of what we are going to do with all of our properties.

With all of that said, starting your home inside of a trust may seem quite advanced, but it is very forward-thinking to the rest of your financial picture. It is an example of a long-term plan if you are thinking about real estate. There are a lot of questions to be answered, such as what are you going to do if and when you die when you own property? Will you occupy, sell, or rent your property? For how long? When will the property need updating and renovations, and what will it cost?

In my opinion, the first professional you should consult with after your education begins (unless you are paying cash) is a loan officer. They can help you to understand what, where, and how you can purchase the property. They may also have other recommendations for financing. Knowing what you can afford is integral to your search. Looking for real estate without a way to pay for it or preapproval is just a waste of your and your real estate agent's time.

Altogether, in the planning stage, it is time to put all that education to good use and envision what your real estate venture is going to look like not just now, but also in the long term.

4. Build A Team

In Chapters 3, 5, and 6, we covered every professional you will want a relationship with when you are renovating a home with renovation loans. It is important that you like the person that you are working with, regardless of whether you are getting "good" or "hard love" back from them. Good teammates will find constructive ways to let you know when you should be making different decisions.

Your team is crucial to your success in renovations, so make sure they are the best team they can be by selecting professionals with whom you have good relationships. Use the tools on thehousehackingbook.com to check off the key professionals you should be acquainting yourself with within your real estate development.

5. Execute

"Analysis paralysis" is a real thing. It is when you get stuck in the education, workup, and consideration of a plan, and then you fail to move forward and do the plan. It can be hard to execute a plan—imagine yourself sitting on the edge of a pool, with your toes in the water, trying to make yourself jump in, and hesitating. However, it is vital not to get caught up in analysis paralysis. You can indeed plan too much and miss out on things like good deals or good timeframes for executing your plan.

Always do your due diligence and get your research done, but when it is done, it is time to move forward. Once you have your plan, your people, and your ideal property, it is time to launch that plan, and move forward on your checklists. It's too easy to second-guess yourself. If your team is all in on your idea, then one of your friends (who doesn't own anything) giving you critique isn't the best sounding board. You've got this! *Execute*!

6. Nurture

Once a project is constructed, it is not complete. Even if you have a property manager, you must constantly monitor things like cash flow, operational costs, upgrades, general maintenance, and vendor relationships. Sometimes the market may yield better rates that improve your cash flow so you must refinance, and sometimes you might even be able to take cash out of your investment to buy more real estate.

You always must keep an eye on your properties to see that things are going well. In other words, you must nurture your investment. This is a never-ending process for as long as you hold real estate. It will not manage itself!

The End Of This Journey, And The Beginning Of The Next

Renovation lending is a revolutionary method of financing great homes. It's the BRRR approach in one step! Whether you are interested in just a single-family home, or you want to go beyond that by getting further into the real estate market by becoming a house hacker, renovation lending has something to offer you. Your dream home is just around the corner, or, if you wish, your dream real estate project can become a reality.

However, you envision your future, renovation lending is a great way to step into real estate. If you have developed an interest in it by reading this book, then I suggest you visit thehousehackingbook.com for further reading and information.

You have reached the end of this book. However, it is not the end of your journey by any means. You see, you have already begun the plan outlined above. Perhaps this is the first book you have read, or perhaps you have read many. Whatever the case, you are conducting your education. Bravo! Great job. Take a breather—you have earned it—and then dive into whatever you have lined up next.

ABOUT THE AUTHOR

John Adams is a real estate investor, top performing renovation loan specialist and instructor for *Distressed Property Solutions & Military Mortgage Boot Camp*. He has been in the real estate industry for almost 20 years working in almost every capacity from being a licensed Agent,

Mortgage Banker to Area Manager. He's been a national top producer recognized for top renovation loan units produced in 2010 through to 2022.

John Adams has spent more than a decade of his career focusing on helping home buyers to use VA Renovation Loans, Fannie Mae Homestyle renovation and FHA 203k renovation loans. He shows clients and agents how to renovate them to their preferences and create wealth in real estate. John has simplified the process that eliminates confusion and time crunches specifically for the processes of Renovation Loans. John Adams and his team can help you turn a bank owned, tired or fixer opportunity property into your dream home and show veterans a better way home.

Made in the USA
Columbia, SC
01 March 2024

32182052R00093